Embracing Disruptive Coherence

Embracing Disruptive Coherence

————— *Coming Out as Erotic Ethical Practice* —————

Kathleen T. Talvacchia

CASCADE *Books* · Eugene, Oregon

EMBRACING DISRUPTIVE COHERENCE
Coming Out as Erotic Ethical Practice

Cascade Books
An Imprint of Wipf and Stock Publishers
199 W. 8th Ave., Suite 3
Eugene, OR 97401

www.wipfandstock.com

PAPERBACK ISBN: 978-1-5326-4888-5
HARDCOVER ISBN: 978-1-5326-4889-2
EBOOK ISBN: 978-1-5326-4890-8

Cataloguing-in-Publication data:

Names: Talvacchia, Kathleen T., author.

Title: Embracing disruptive coherence : coming out as erotic ethical practice / by Kathleen T. Talvacchia.

Description: Eugene, OR : Cascade Books, 2019 | Includes bibliographical references.

Identifiers: ISBN 978-1-5326-4888-5 (paperback) | ISBN 978-1-5326-4889-2 (hardcover) | ISBN 978-1-5326-4890-8 (ebook)

Subjects: LCSH: Coming Out (Sexual Orientation). | Bible—Gay interpretations. | Queer theology—Criticism and interpretation. | Gender identity. | Homosexuality—Religious aspects—Christianity.

Classification: BT708 .T34 2019 (print) | BT708 .T34 (ebook)

Manufactured in the U.S.A.   04/16/19

For my parents and parents-in-law from whom I learned
the wisdom and power of disruption and coherence

Contents

Preface

This book has been at least thirty years in the making. Or at least it feels that way to me. I have wrestled over the years to understand what the process of coming out means as an idea, but, more importantly, as a reality of lived experience for myself and other LGBTIQ persons. Coming out was an intensely transformative process for me, grounded in the spiritual practices of my Catholic Christian tradition. It was a major disruption that also provided a profound sense of coherence. I puzzled to understand how it could be both, and yet, it was true to my experience. At the same time, coming out has placed me in certain boxes that I have long resisted. Often, I felt that only some of me was permitted to be part of a visible lesbian identification. Through much trial and error, I grappled with negotiating the fluidity of disclosure and hiddenness that both protected me and compromised me. And yet, more often I experienced an empowerment and cohesion that came from being able to manifest and live out an aspect about myself—certainly in motion and developing over time—that felt authentic and real. I know that these experiences are not unique to me. I was drawn to understand on a theological and spiritual level the energy that made the coming out process so intensely compelling.

Coming out, a term of identity politics that expressed the revealing of gender and sexual non-normativity, has been problematized for good reason. Historically it represented a fixed and stable identity, hidden until a personal enlightenment, a hidden essence that finally came into awareness, could be made visible. Once visible, it was a repetition of a specific revelation, in which a coming out story defined and explained one's experience and identity. It was considered a binary reality—one was either in or out. As a stable identity, it could overshadow other contextual experiences that were part of one's privilege or marginalization in an unjust society.

The advent of postmodernist thinking upended fixed and stabilized understandings of contextually-based identities, blurring traditional understandings of gender and sexuality in order to articulate its fluidity and movement. Coming out as it had been understood theoretically was not helpful and, certainly, problematic. At the same time, in parts of the United States and other areas of the world, LGBTIQ identifications were becoming more accepted, although not for all persons whose contextual realities exposed them to biases in addition to gender and sexuality discrimination. The phrase "coming out" then took on a new problem. It was associated with actions of assimilation into an unjust social structure. If one had the privilege of living in a social context, or working in a job, or participating in a religious tradition where lesbian, gay, or bisexual identifications were accepted, then coming out seemed to pose minimal risk. Worse, it made it possible to be satisfied with the status quo and ignore the injustices that other groups experienced. Once and for all, it seemed that the phrase "coming out" ought to fade into its historically specific context.

With all its baggage and problems, why would I want to think about coming out? The answer, although simple in its statement, is exceedingly complicated in reality. The intersectionality of multiple identifications, often lived in the middle spaces between disclosure and hiddenness, show that negotiating the revelations of coming out is still a reality for many. Heteronormative structures persist and pose concrete consequences that require navigation. For persons and groups that experience the multiple social marginalization of race, class, disability status, religious affiliation, immigration status, and ethnic culture, the revelations involved in coming out are real and complicated.

I also realized that outside of academic circles the phrase was not only still in use to describe experiences of gender and sexual differences but was often used contextually beyond issues of gender and sexuality. It could be used in these ways to speak about a person's or group's social difference from communal definitions of what was considered normal and their demands for justice and inclusion. Coming out, for example, as a person with disabilities, or as a survivor of assault, or as a person in substance abuse recovery was part of language and culture in many situations. Furthermore, I realized that these experiences of coming out were articulated in ways that showed them to empower and support persons and groups in their struggle to fight the targeting of bias, discrimination, and invisibility that they experienced. From my own experience of coming out, I have some insight into these experiences of "coming out."

Coming out as it had been understood had been important—even life-saving—yet, it needed to be reimagined. It needed to be unsettled, troubled, and destabilized. It needed to be queered. Just as the word "queer" had been reclaimed from a term of contempt to a term of empowerment, I wanted to see if the phrase "coming out" could be reimagined to express the life-giving force that I saw in others and experienced in my own life. I came to see that the power of coming out was not in revealing an identity. Its transformative energy was more properly an ethical practice—the ethical practice of truth-telling.

In this project I am using certain words that, within the complications inherent to re-imagining a new understanding of coming out, might be confusing. I want to take a moment to briefly clarify my queer reading of these words as a way of articulating the parameters of the work. Even though I am talking about truth-telling, I do not understand it to be speaking of a "Truth" that is essentialized. I see truth-telling as part of an ongoing process of enacting a person's or a group's becoming in their communal, social, political, and economic relationships. In that regard I prefer to use the term becoming-selfhood-in-relation to speak about an emerging and ongoing sense of authenticity or realness about one's developing selfhood. In addition, in an effort to both signify many fluid identifications by using the word "queer," and honoring particular histories, struggles, and experiences that lesbian, gay, bisexual, transgender, intersex, and queer persons have, I use both designations intentionally. Finally, while I refer to specific ideas from queer theorists, this project is not an argument in the field of queer theory. It is more properly a work of queer theology from the perspective of a Christian-based practical theology and ethics.

The process of research and writing this book brought new vigor to my sense that coming out can be once again an important way to think about lives that transgress the normative discourse of a community. For me its energy lies in an openness to embrace the fear and exhilaration of truth-telling.

Acknowledgments

A significant portion of the research for this book was done while I was a Visiting Research Scholar at Union Theological Seminary in 2016 and Spring 2017. I would like to express my appreciation to President Serene Jones and Vice-President of Academic Affairs and Dean Mary C. Boys for their support of this work. My thanks also go to Matthew Baker, Director of the Burke Library at Union for his help with resources for research.

My heartfelt appreciation goes to colleagues and friends who read portions of the manuscript in draft form and provided important feedback and support: Sarah Azaransky, Marvin Ellison, Brigitte Kahl, and Jan Rehmann. I am also deeply grateful to colleagues and friends who talked over ideas with me and provided helpful insights and suggested resources to consider: Beth Bidlack, Rita Nakashima Brock, Cláudio Carvalhaes, Patrick Cheng, Pamela Cooper-White, Bruce Grant, Lea Matthews, Cameron Partridge, Lisa Thompson, and Nikki Young. I am blessed that I had the opportunity to discuss my ideas and research for this book with James H. Cone in the year before his passing. I am grateful for his wisdom and insight.

I send my deepest love and gratitude to all of the members of the Talvacchia Family for their interest in the project and support along the way. Your love and care has sustained me over all my years in so many ways, and for that I am truly thankful. My love also to the Pak Family for their support and encouragement. I feel very lucky to be related to all of you.

To my children Jocelyn and Chloe and my son-in-law Patrick, your support and care have filled my heart with happiness. I am so impressed with the people that you have become and the lives you lead. I hope that I can keep up! A special word of thanks to Jocelyn who did a terrific job getting the manuscript ready for submission.

I am tremendously blessed to have a partner who is also an intellectual companion. Su's patient listening to my jumbled thoughts, her insightful analysis of my ideas (or lack thereof), her rigorous critiques and enthusiastic affirmations of my drafts, and, of course, her wisdom to know when I needed a good push, has made all the difference. We have walked a precious journey together for which I feel profound thankfulness.

1

Coming Out Matters

*I*s it necessary to come out? My partner, Su, and I debated this very real question together as we thought about how to accommodate the fact of my parents-in-law coming to live with us in our home. At that point, our lives as an interracial queer couple had been firmly and openly established both professionally and personally. We had been together for close to a decade, were deeply involved in our respective families, raising two children and had bought a house. Yet, we approached this discussion negotiating the messiness of lived experience where theory and practice collide and reflected-upon judgment becomes the map that guides you safely through to the place where you can put your feet down, if imperfectly, in stable and consistent action.

My parents-in-law, Korean immigrants who had been in the United States for close to forty years by then as citizens of this country, lived in a world in which queer lives were not visibly present. Their evangelical Christianity had negative opinions about LGBTQI life, but mostly it was not something that they felt was in their world. In whatever way they understood my relationship with their daughter, it did not include the idea of the two of us being a couple.

As Su and I reflected upon our situation and discussed possible actions to live in a peaceful environment of family care, we sought to balance both the context of our relationship—one that we had nurtured with great intention amid the pressures of a white-dominant, heteronormative society, and one that we wanted to continue to grow and thrive—and the context of our elders, who struggled with the effects of Korean historical traumas, illness, aging, and the ongoing injustices of racism and xenophobia. The intersectionality of gender, sexuality, culture, history, immigration experience, and religion grounded us in multiple discourses of power that became a part of

1

the boundaries we drew and the complexity that we embraced.[1] It required that we engage a "critical mind and a discerning heart,"[2] to understand both the reality of discourses of social power that were operating in the situation and the personal experiences of all involved. We were not only persons who were affected by the identification categories of social difference, but human beings with history together who cared about each other's well-being.

We came to clarity about a way to proceed when we centered ourselves on an important insight: even though there was much we did not know about how to handle this situation, we knew we were responsible to live truthful lives. The complexity of living this truth meant honoring the authenticity of our life as a couple and not forcing our elders to completely live in our reality. We determined, then, to live openly as a couple, while not ever explicitly sitting them down to explain in detail what they were witnessing. We would live as authentically as possible, and if they asked specifically, then we would talk about our relationship directly. It became apparent after a time that my father-in-law, without speaking to us about it, understood the nature of our relationship. My mother-in-law, in the early stages of Alzheimer's disease, did not seem to notice or care about her Italian-American "daughter's" relationship with her own daughter.

There may have been other solutions, but for us this type of coming out provided a way to accommodate many of the needs of the persons involved and respect the contexts of our lived experience. This solution was entirely different, for example, from the decision we had made in dealing with my father as he aged (my mother had passed many years earlier). We were involved in his elder years with a very different set of circumstances, including the fact that he did not live with us. Su and I were out to him very explicitly to the point that I was able to have conversations with him about marriage equality and our life as a couple. Yet, there were times when we were introduced to his friends or medical caretakers that we were not introduced as a couple, nor did we necessarily appear that way.

While in one context (my father) our coming out was more overt and in another (my parents-in-law) our coming out was subtler, in both cases coming out was a fluid negotiation in each moment of balancing authenticity with the need to move through the social world with a strategic sense of both effectiveness and personal survival. Both circumstances hinged on the practices of truth-telling that allowed us to live authentic lives.

1. Pak, "Coming Home/Coming Out," 337–52.
2. Talvacchia, *Critical Minds and Discerning Hearts.*

2

Anyone who has come out and lives a life that transgresses the gender expectations of heteronormative society understands that a coming-out experience is not a once-for-all reality. Rather, in many important ways coming out means knowing when not to be out. By this I mean that in the practices of everyday living queer people often need to navigate through heteronormative power structures that negatively affect them with the wisdom and agility that both protects from harm and empowers authenticity. Success depends on embracing a fluid understanding of the constant movement between being out and being in the closet, disclosure and hiddenness, revelation and covering.

This book developed out of my desire to understand what has been for me an enduring question for the over thirty years in which I have lived an openly lesbian life: What is the place of truth-telling in the fluidity of the coming-out process? Engaging this question with integrity and intellectual rigor requires that we acknowledge and accept the personal and social responsibility of just action with an awareness of the structures of power that inhibit and discipline our capacity to live fully in the freedom we seek.

But the need to reconsider coming out and truth-telling is more than a persistent personal question. Theories of gender, sexuality, and queerness interrogate what it means to live as a gender minority in a heteronormative society and have proposed many important critiques about the traditional ways that we have thought about coming out. (I will discuss this in more detail in the third chapter.) Yet, in the practices of queer living the need to come out remains consistent in many different contexts. Coming out is a real experience for many LGBTQI persons. This was evident, for example, in the aftermath of the tragedy at the Orlando nightclub in which 49 LGBTQI persons, a large majority of whom were Latino/a,[3] were killed.[4] For many of the victims, those who perished and

3. I am using the form Latino/a to be consistent with the terminology used by the journalist who reported the story for *The New York Times* (for citation, see note 4). It is important to note that among many persons of Latin American heritage there is an increasing preference for the term Latinx, rather than Latino/a or Latin@, as a means of challenging the gendered nature of the Spanish language and, thereby creating more inclusivity for transgendered and gender-fluid persons in the community. For a helpful overview of the debate, see María Scharrón-del Río and Alan A. Aja, "The Case FOR 'Latinx': Why Intersectionality Is Not a Choice," *Latino Rebels*, December 5, 2015. Also, for more information about the prevalence of Latino/a victims in the massacre, see Lizette Alvarez and Nick Madigan, "In the Dead in Orlando, Puerto Ricans Hear a Roll Call of their Kin," *The New York Times*, June 14, 2016.

4. Julie Turkewitz, "Orlando Massacre Inspires Some to Come Out as Gay," *The New York Times*, June 21, 2016.

those who survived, it was a moment that communicated a fundamental fact about their lives to their families who did not know.[5] What does coming out and truth-telling mean in the context of transgressive ways of theorizing gender, sexuality, and queerness in a social context in which compelling theoretical ideas can at times diverge with the practical realities of cultural contexts and positionality?

Finally, the enormous social changes regarding LGBTQI experience in the past fifty years necessitate a rethinking about what it means to come out. We remember the fiftieth anniversary of the Compton's Cafeteria riots (1966)[6] and we look forward to the fiftieth anniversary of the Stonewall riots (1969).[7] These important historical markers ignited a movement to push for greater visibility, acceptance, and inclusion of LGBTQI persons in US society. Because cultural perspectives have changed in that time, coming out looks very different now than it did in previous decades. We now live in a country that upholds marriage equality and provides in many states legal recourse to combat homophobic discrimination or hate crimes.[8] At the same time, gains that have been established in support of LGBTQI civil rights and social acceptance have been contested or reversed.[9] Proposed or established laws that target transgendered persons or that seek to permit discrimination based on gender and sexual identity are being actively debated, enacted, and then, repealed.[10] Despite the astonishing

5. "Some had their sexuality revealed by accident: Gertrude Merced learned that her 25-year-old son, Enrique, was gay only after she heard the news of his death. Others, though, have chosen to expose their inner lives, stirred by the outpouring of support for Orlando's gay community or wrought with sorrow and unable to keep their secrets anymore." Turkewitz, *The New York Times*, June 21, 2016.

6. For more information, see Ryan Kost, "The Riot that Predated Stonewall, 50 Years Later," *San Francisco Chronicle*, June 25, 2016; Nicole Pasulka, "Ladies in the Streets: Before Stonewall, Transgender Uprising Changed Lives," *NPR*, May 5, 2015; documentary film, *Screaming Queens: The Riot at Compton's Cafeteria* (2005).

7. For more on the Stonewall Riots see Carter, *Stonewall* and Duberman, *Stonewall*.

8. See the Human Rights Campaign's webpage "Maps of State Laws and Policies" www.hrc.org/state_maps.

9. See, for example, Jennifer Finney Boylan, "Is America Growing Less Tolerant on L.G.B.T.Q. Rights," *New York Times*, January 29, 2018, and "Despite Gains, LGBT Protections Remain a Patchwork in the U.S.," by The Associated Press as reported in *The New York Times*, April 5, 2017. For an analysis of political backlash against LGBTQI civil rights, see Richard Socarides, "North Carolina and the Gay Rights Backlash," *The New Yorker*, March 28, 2016, and "North Carolina 'Bathroom Bill' Reset Gets Applause and Jeers," by The Associated Press, as reported in *The New York Times*, April 1, 2017.

10. For an historical overview of contested debates surrounding LGBTQI civil

social changes of the past fifty years that have created more inclusivity and acceptance, many queers—especially trans persons[11]—experience violence, harassment, discrimination, community and familial rejection, and religious condemnation.[12] What does coming out and truth-telling mean in this contested landscape of both legal protections and societal and communal backlash?

These questions form the basis of assumptions that I bring to this work. On personal, academic, and social grounds, coming out matters to many people and in many communities. It matters because truth-telling matters when we are faced with the need to affirm an undeniable aspect of our self that transgresses religious or social normative boundaries. To affirm a transgressive identity makes us vulnerable, but to constantly deny, evade, or cover an authentic self-identification holds the potential to destroy our ethical center, which guides our judgment and directs our moral action.

I assert that the practice of truth-telling can be a lens through which we can examine coming out theologically and morally. It permits an understanding of coming out that views it as a fluid process of negotiating the complexity of living a personal authenticity while resisting systems of power that seek to punish transgressive action. Specifically, I argue that rather than the declaration of an identity category, coming out can be understood as the erotic ethical practice of truth-telling, which is developed through the formation of conscience and the practice of discernment. The ethical practice of coming out articulates actions that are erotic, that is,

protections, see "Understanding Transgender Access Laws," *The New York Times*, February 24, 2017. For helpful analysis, see Jeannie Suk Gersen's series of articles for *The New Yorker*, posted on NewYorker.com: "The Transgender Bathroom Debate and the Looming Title IX Crisis," May 24, 2016; "Gavin Grimm's Transgender-Rights Case and the Problem with Informal Executive Action," December 6, 2016; "A Moment of Uncertainty for Transgender Rights," February 27, 2017; "A New Phase of Chaos on Transgender Rights," March 13, 2017.

11. See the Human Rights Campaign's webpage "Addressing Anti-Transgender Violence—Exploring Realities, Challenges and Solutions." http://www.hrc.org/resources/addressing-anti-transgender-violence-exploring-realities-challenges-and-sol.

12. For more information, see Haeyoun Park and Iaryna Mykhyalyshyn, "LGBT People Are More Likely to Be Targets of Hate Crimes Than Any Other Minority Group," *The New York Times*, June 16, 2016; Emma Green, "The Extraordinarily Common Violence Against LGBT People in America," *The Atlantic*, June 12, 2016; Mark Potok, "Anti-Gay Crimes: Doing the Math," Southern Poverty Law Center—Intelligence Report, February 27, 2011; Michelle A. Marzulllo and Alyn J. Libman, "Research Overview: Hate Crimes and Violence against Lesbian, Gay, Bisexual and Transgender People," Human Rights Campaign, 2009.

based in our bodies, passions, and sensuality. Communities of religious practice rooted in a religious tradition, as well as family and social culture, help to shape moral conscience. Discernment, both individual and communal, makes space in those communities for transgressive truth to be embraced intentionally. This perspective allows for a different kind of conversation about coming out that makes space for both important theoretical perspectives that challenge rigid or binary constructions of identity and the lived experiences of persons and communities who negotiate the nuances of those identifications in a world of relationships, cultures, and personal and social costs. When understood as the erotic ethical practice of truth-telling, coming out empowers a subjectivity that allows a personal or communal truth to challenge structures of normalization that deny an authentic human freedom.

Coming out as truth-telling embraces both actions of disruption that queer and destabilize established gender norms, and actions creating coherence that solidifies a subjective identification of becoming-selfhood-in-relation. Each action has its own integrity within a synergistic relationship—disruption unsettles coherence and opens it to further development, and coherence gathers together multiple identifications to help create a sense of clarity and perspective. The energy of disruption, when wielded as a positive desire for growth and development, has the potential to shake up established understandings and bring in new ways of engaging diversity and establishing inclusion. The energy of establishing coherence, when wielded as consolidation without homogenization, empowers queer bodies with the freedom to live with passion and personal integrity. These combined energies, which I am calling disruptive coherence, create a vision of coming out that is both disorderly and integrative, prophetic and truthful. Embracing disruptive coherence becomes the action of queer empowerment and justice.

I want to state several boundaries of this project at the outset to clarify both its intentions as well as its limits. First, while theories of gender identity and performativity influence how or even whether we speak about coming out, this book does not focus on those matters specifically. On the level of theoretical analysis alone one might reasonably assert that if gender is a socially constructed performativity, coming out is obsolete and, therefore, unnecessary to examine. Although important to consider, this project arises from my focus on the lived experience of queer persons where coming out remains an insistent and urgent reality. Because that urgency and lived reality is compelling to me, I seek a different conversation in which coming out is examined as an ethical practice of queer lives.

Second, my own positionality as a Christian—rooted in both the traditions of my progressive Roman Catholic identity and my long association professionally in liberal Protestant, ecumenical, and interfaith academic contexts—influences my understanding of practices and the role it might play in coming out. While I seek in this work to transcend these limitations as appropriate, Christian discourses ground my thinking in important ways and shape the ideas that follow.

Third, while I seek to propose a way of thinking about coming out that will be generalizable beyond the limitations of specific experiences, I am not seeking to construct a systematic way to understand all experiences of transgressive gender identification. As a queer theologian who studies the practices, dispositions, and habits of Christian religious communities, I pay specific scholarly attention to the ways in which theory, lived experience, and reflected-upon practice engage in the creative solution of a compelling communal problem. This project represents an exercise in constructive queer theology in which I am reflecting upon a critical experience of many queer communities, and then using those insights to develop broader statements about what might be considered consistent communal practices that make sense within specific cultural contexts. These consistent communal practices hold the capacity to express communal identities in the contexts of their location to discourses of power and in their relation to the larger religious traditions of which they are members. Thus, as I am reflecting upon coming out as the erotic ethical practice of truth-telling, I am also thinking about how the practices of Christian communities in various cultural contexts might support and sustain such truth-telling. At the same time, I leave space in the conversation for those communities or persons for whom coming out is not possible (for reasons such as potential bodily harm or severe cost that is not sustainable), or not so urgent, or for whom understanding it as an ethical practice might not make sense in their context.

While this current chapter makes the case for why coming out still matters in the lives of many queer persons, the second chapter provides a different perspective on this claim. It explores reflections on a biblical text that can provide a spiritual grounding for the meaningfulness of coming out experiences. Through a queer reading of the text, which is engaged with queer experiences, it suggests how these passages might provide insight about a spiritual understanding of coming out and its place in queer lives.

Having explored some experiential base points about coming out, the first two chapters provide the foundation of critical thinking and discerning compassion that represents the core of my way of doing practical theology and approaching the complex fluidity and nuances in the dynamic of disclosure and hiddenness. (As the popular saying goes, "It's complicated!")

The third chapter makes the case for erotic ethical practice as a way to think about coming out. This chapter creates a rationale for using practices as an interpretive lens and situates the conversation in the literature and discussions of queer theory, queer theology, and religious practices. It establishes connections between truth-telling, the erotic, knowledge, and power.

The fourth chapter develops the basic scaffolding of the concept of disruptive coherence. It develops the connections between the erotic, truth-telling, and ethical practices of disruptive coherence. An important aspect of the argument involves making the case for the necessity of an internal ethical conviction that can ground a statement of truth strong enough to oppose societal and religious norms that deny the full humanity of queer persons. This requires the use of moral judgment, which is developed through conscience formation and the practice of discernment.

The heart of the book is the fifth chapter, which explains the idea of coming out as the erotic ethical practice of disruptive coherence in lived experience. The realities of both disruption and coherence are defined and distinguished, with emphasis on both its positive and negative aspects. Critical ideas of normativity and power are placed in conversation with both conscience and discernment to understand the transgressive center of the coming-out process, as well as moral and strategic ways to express truth-telling.

The final chapter concludes that, understood as disruptive coherence, coming out is an erotic ethical practice of justice, engaging a becoming-selfhood-in-relation in community in a way that works to build a more diverse and inclusive society, and thus, is a prophetic action on behalf of justice. Religious communities, then, should embrace coming out as a transformative practice.

Now that I have stated the argument and sketched the outline of the book, 1 will turn to exploring aspects of coming out from the experiential starting point of engaging the complexity and contested categories of queer lives.

Engaging Queer Lives: Intersectionality and Coming Out

The process of coming out grounds us communally in several ways: we come out from the communities that shaped us, enter diverse LGBTQI communities and, for many, live in opposition to communities (sometimes our own) with norms that do not accept queer identities. Sometimes we move fluidly between those communities. In these circumstances, we necessarily engage the truth-telling of coming out in dialogue with those communities with whom we are in conflict.

Because coming out matters for many in queer lived experience, it also matters that we have a way to embrace its empowerment—one that honors the intricacies of living out truth amid intersecting discourses of social power. That complexity is often best understood through an analysis of experiences in which our social identities collide, and borders are crossed, exposing areas in which we benefit from societal privilege, endure the effects of societal punishment, or some combination of benefits and negative effect. Intersectionality—the intersecting and overlapping of multiple social identities that reveal complex structures of power and marginalization—exposes many of the realities that make coming out a fluid action of disclosure and hiddenness.[13] Awareness of the ways that multiple social identifications and their effects exist in queer communities centers a discussion of coming out in that very real negotiation.

Jasbir K. Puar raises an important criticism about intersectionality that I find useful for understanding its function as a lived reality. She challenges the ways in which intersectionality, based in models of identity politics, assumes that categories of social identity are distinct and can be separated from each other. In this way, intersectional analysis creates essentialist categories of identity that do not represent the complexity of queer experiences; these are then used within systems of social power to manage and control diverse communities. Instead she advocates for the concept of assemblages as a category that acknowledges the instability of the multiple realities that make up a group, destabilizes representational identities and, therefore, allows for the fluidity, contingency, and messiness that queerness

13. Nancy Ramsay understands intersectionality as "a theory that helps students and faculty better understand and engage with the complex, constructed, and intersecting simultaneity of identity and its entanglement with asymmetries of power." See Ramsay, "Intersectionality and Theological Education," 7. Robyn Henderson-Espinoza seeks to move beyond representational limitations of intersectionality using the concept of interconnectivity. See Henderson-Espinoza, "Thinking at the Intersections," 11.

encompasses.[14] However, despite this preference for assemblages, she acknowledges the limitations of its uses as an analytic category. For Puar, given the reality and persistence of the social categories of difference that intersectionality analyzes, and the use of these categories by power structures to control social groups, "intersectional identities and assemblages must remain as interlocutors in tension."[15]

Thus, any discussion of intersectionality and coming out must account for the destabilized fluidity of identities and avoid stereotypes of identity categories in which complex social groups and the individuals that comprise them are fossilized into rigid essences. It must equally attend to how these complex identities engage structures of power that have privileging or disciplining effects.

Patricia Hill Collins and Sirma Bilge provide a useful approach that seeks to avoid the problem of essentialism in traditional intersectional analysis and to provide a clear articulation of the social location of lived experiences and its effects. They understand intersectionality to have the following core ideas that center its concerns: social inequality, relationality, power both in the intersection of social locations of difference and across domains (personal, structural, culture, norms), social context, complexity, and social justice. Within this framework, when considered as a theoretical category of analysis alone, intersectionality can fall into the problems of fixed and stable categories of identity. However, they critique such approaches as disconnected from the critical reflection on experience that occurs in communities and individuals, which highlights their particularities and nuances and have the capacity to challenge essentialized representations of identities.[16] Relationality is fundamental in their understanding: there is "a synergistic relationship joining intersectionality as a form of critical inquiry and praxis."[17] Thus, they argue that the critical inquiry of intersectionality must be paired with an awareness of the critical praxis of communities. This approach—combining critical inquiry with critical praxis—provides a necessary foundation for a discussion of the lived experiences of the coming out process within an intersectional framework.

14. Puar, *Terrorist Assemblages*, 211–16.
15. Puar, *Terrorist Assemblages*, 213.
16. Collins and Bilge, *Intersectionality*, 25–31.
17. Collins and Bilge, *Intersectionality*, 48.

Intersectionality in a Queer Family Context

With these caveats in mind, let me return to the story that begins this chapter about living with our elders to reflect more deeply upon the complexity of intersectionality and the fluid truth-telling of coming out. As I stated earlier, Su and I understood truth-telling to be the core conviction that guided our actions, the moral issue that embodied "the heart of the matter" in our dilemma. Yet, we knew that living out that truth-telling placed our actions in the messy realm of social contexts, cultures, and lived experience—within which we faced overlapping levels of discrimination and marginalization. Understanding those standpoints, their implications on our lives and our elders' lives, as well as the costs associated with any option before us, became the raw materials of our decision-making process.

In writing about the complexity of negotiating the disclosure of our queer relationship within the overlapping pressures of race, immigration, religion, culture, sexuality, and gender, Su writes about the "vertiginal movements" she experienced as primary caretaker of her parents, and that we experienced together as a queer couple:

> Negotiating the degrees of "outness" is a delicate dance that requires thought, judgement, and begs the question "what is the purpose of coming out in this situation?" To my siblings, I am out. To my parents' primary doctor, I am out. My cousins—out. My aunts and uncles—not out (though I suspect my aunt knows). To the Medicaid case worker—out. Korean home care—not out. My parents' church friends and pastors—not out. I constantly ask myself, how will it affect the care of my mother by me being out? And this is further complicated because this has to be negotiated in our own space called home. . . . While coming home for my parents dragged me home to a place I left many years ago, for Kathy, it made home a strange place where she was at times, "the girl who lived upstairs."[18]

Several social positionalities collided here, requiring authentic disclosure to be mediated in conversation with the probable cost for her parents' care, for her as a Korean American and for us as an interracial queer couple.

What does justice demand in this situation? Christian stances ground action for justice in the dignity of the human person and in a preferential option for the marginalized and structurally disempowered. Acting justly demanded that we consider solutions that would maintain the integrity of

18. Pak, "Coming Home/Coming Out," 340.

our relationship and, at the same time, protect it from racist and homophobic social forces that are directed at ensuring that relationships such as ours falter through a constant denial of their validity and, thus, rendering them illegitimate and invisible.

However, acting justly also demanded that we consider solutions that would respect the physical stamina, the emotional fortitude, the traumatic scars (endured from both Korean history and immigrant experiences of racism and xenophobia), and the willing sacrifices that our elders carried with them and into our home. Justice also demanded that we bring into our reflections the values associated with our Italian and Korean ethnic cultures, with their emphasis on the creation and sustaining of families, the protection and support of family bonds, and the responsibility to care for elders.

We also thought about the larger social issues of care for elders, particularly when they have lived through immigrant experiences as racial ethnic minorities. It was all too obvious to us that our elders, through aging and infirmity, had lost their capacity to function effectively in their adopted social context. The personal and communal resources they possessed that helped them cope with immigrant life were not as available to them at this stage of their lives. We knew we were not alone in this dilemma. Sitting in the New York City waiting rooms of their gerontologists, we saw the social issues starkly: rooms filled with middle-aged children (mostly women) and their elderly parents and family members, many from immigrant communities, negotiating language, the health care system, and cultural norms. In what ways were we a part of this larger social concern? How would the decisions we made be affected by these larger social structures?

We arrived at the decision of how to act only after we understood with sufficient clarity the depth of the overlapping systems of discrimination and disadvantage operating in our context (both for our elders and for us), and then put them in conversation with our Christian religious values. We came to see that an understanding of intersectionality in the context of queerness created the freedom to engage the wisdom of our moral tradition so that we could understand the ways in which our truth-telling could be authentic and, yet, aware of the factors of discrimination that moderate *how* that truth-telling is expressed.

Thus, coming out continues to matter—both in practice in queer life and as a concept for queer theological reflection—because queer people continue to live in an intersectional reality, in which the persistence of discriminations and disadvantages against minoritized social groups collides with their queerness. And because it continues to matter in queer lives, it is an important subject of queer theologizing. Coming out is the erotic ethical practice of truth-telling that negotiates queer authenticity within the very real consequences of social discourses of power that are being directed at members of society who embody a subjugated difference, and who live the consequences of that devaluation. Queerness can intersect with one's privileges as well as disempowerments. Understanding the dynamic of privilege and disempowerment must be present in negotiating the rigors of coming out amid the presence of white-dominant, ableist, heteronormative, gender-normative, and transphobic social realties.

Because of the complex effects of social power impacting the diversity of queer identities, coming out—as a concrete experience in queer lives and not as a "so-called-experience"—deserves renewed attention. The fluid movement, related to our social contexts, that characterizes the dynamic motion of negotiating the many nuances of being out and being in the closet, disclosure and hiddenness, revelation and covering challenge essentialist binary constructions. In the end, these movements seek to make sense of how we can relate to others and with integrity. How do we relate to where we came from? How do we relate to where we are going? These are the explorations of what coming out as disruptive coherence means. These questions are practically significant and ethically imperative, but also deeply involved with our sense of God in our queer lives.

2

Queer Lives and Biblical Reflections on Coming Out

The previous chapter makes the claim that in the lived experience of many queer persons, coming out matters deeply and has real consequences in their lives. As such, coming out needs to be recovered as a topic of queer theological inquiry. Through a critical intersectional analysis of negotiating the complexity and nuances of a coming-out experience in my life, I sought to pose the problem and offer a way to consider coming out that is not attached to essentialist identity categories. In proposing coming out as an ethical practice, I am seeking to honor the role that coming out can play for queer persons in living lives of integrity.

In this chapter I want to consider queer lives from a different perspective that reflects upon queer engagement with religious traditions through sacred Scripture. Through a theological reflection process[1] using a Christian biblical text, I hope to provide another way to think about coming out that is grounded in the action of truth-telling.

While coming-out experiences are concrete, embodied, and consequential in a heteronormative, homophobic, and transphobic society, they contain spiritual and relational realities as well. These aspects of experience are focused on human spirit and the inner dimension of persons in community with the sacred and all living things. The process of coming out provides clarity about *how* we can love others authentically as sexual beings who love physically, emotionally, and spiritually in queer ways. This desire-knowledge becomes known in our relationships; for many LGBTQI persons, that relational knowledge of embodied loving extends to our

---

1. For more information and an example of a theological reflection process, see Talvacchia, "Disrupting the Theory-Practice Binary," 184–94.

engagement with the divine, the sacred—to God. These relations are in the category of our spiritual connectedness to God, and to the communities, religious traditions, and the sacred texts of those traditions in which we find God. Together, queer sexuality and queer spirituality animate meaning-making in queer lives.

Because the Bible has been used against LGBTQI persons, it is necessary for queer religious persons to claim their own readings of the biblical tradition.[2] In this chapter I seek to engage in my own "taking back" of the Scriptures and engage in a queer reading of a text that has meaning for me as one that speaks to an experience of coming out.[3] As a queer religious person rooted in the Christian tradition, sacred texts from the Bible ground my relational engagement with God, providing insight and meaning in my queer experiences. Focusing on the story of Jesus' rejection at Nazareth in the Gospel of Luke (4:16–30), I engage in a queer reading of the text from a queer sensibility that is informed by my context, positionality, and experience. For me, this queer reading destabilizes the conventional readings of the text and offers new meanings for queer religious experiences. I offer it not as a way of creating a normative reading, or as reflective of the experiences of all queer Christians, or as a prescriptive articulation of queer truth-telling, but, rather, as an example of how queer experience and Christian texts might be in conversation in a way that *values* queer lived experience.

Before I begin, though, I want to clarify the way in which I am engaging the biblical text. Practical theology is a contextual way of "doing" theology—a method that seeks to examine and understand ways to live authentically within a tradition. Within the field of practical theology, scholarly reflection often builds upon the exegetical work of biblical scholars to engage the texts in dialogue with the lived experiences of religious persons and communities. The intent of using Scripture in practical theology is to provide insight and meaning into the lived reality of embodied faith. The exegesis engages biblical scholarship of the scriptural text along with the human text of faith experiences in order to understand how these two texts can speak to each other and mutually inform both interpretation and action.

2. See, for example, Guest et al., *Queer Bible Commentary*.

3. I am using the imagery of "taking back" from Goss and West, *Take Back the Word*.

Paul Ballard provides a helpful overview of the ways in which the Bible "can and should" be used in this way of doing theology.[4] One mode, "The Bible as a Resource," begins from a situation and then moves to use the Bible as a resource that can illuminate and deepen experience; this is most clearly seen in pastoral care and counseling activities. Another mode, "Working from the Bible," centers the Bible within a community in which, "Christian identity is openly acknowledged and the congregation and individuals place themselves deliberately before God, who is mediated in and through the Bible."[5] This mode is clearly represented in the worship and spirituality of a religious tradition. A third mode, "The Bible as Wisdom," uses the Bible in theological reflection, the method by which religious tradition and lived experience are engaged in critical dialogue. For Ballard, the "critical dialogue between present reality and tradition . . . is the heart of practical theological method."[6] Ballard reserves as a concluding point a use of Scripture that he believes needs greater development. In the final mode, "Discovering the Bible," practical theology should develop empirical and evaluative research that can ascertain how the Bible is received and used in the world. He suggests, for example, research that considers how lay persons read Scripture, or ways that the Bible is used in congregational worship, and how the Bible is engaged in postmodern culture as important areas of inquiry.

This reading uses Ballard's mode of "The Bible as Wisdom" to engage a queer reading of the Lukan text. Present reality and Christian traditions are placed in critical dialogue in this theological reflection to gain insight and meaning for queer Christian lives. The text, Luke 4:16–30, is useful for reflection because it presents a vivid story of truth-telling in one's home community about an identification of becoming-selfhood-in-relation that challenges established social and religious norms. The text has dynamics that may be recognizable in many (although, not all) queer experiences of coming out. What can queer persons learn and understand about their lives from this story about Jesus? Can reflecting on this text from the perspective of queer experiences provide biblical wisdom to *support and sustain* coming out?

4. Ballard, "Use of Scripture," 165.
5. Ballard, "Use of Scripture," 167.
6. Ballard, "Use of Scripture," 168.

The Rejection of Jesus at Nazareth—Luke 4:16–30 NRSV

¹⁶ When he came to Nazareth, where he had been brought up, he went to the synagogue on the sabbath day, as was his custom. He stood up to read, ¹⁷ and the scroll of the prophet Isaiah was given to him. He unrolled the scroll and found the place where it was written:

> ¹⁸ "The Spirit of the Lord is upon me,
> because he has anointed me
> to bring good news to the poor.
> He has sent me to proclaim release to the captives
> and recovery of sight to the blind,
> to let the oppressed go free,
> ¹⁹ to proclaim the year of the Lord's favor."

²⁰ And he rolled up the scroll, gave it back to the attendant, and sat down. The eyes of all in the synagogue were fixed on him. ²¹ Then he began to say to them, "Today this scripture has been fulfilled in your hearing." ²² All spoke well of him and were amazed at the gracious words that came from his mouth. They said, "Is not this Joseph's son?" ²³ He said to them, "Doubtless you will quote to me this proverb, 'Doctor, cure yourself!' And you will say, 'Do here also in your hometown the things that we have heard you did at Capernaum.'" ²⁴ And he said, "Truly I tell you, no prophet is accepted in the prophet's hometown. ²⁵ But the truth is, there were many widows in Israel in the time of Elijah, when the heaven was shut up three years and six months, and there was a severe famine over all the land; ²⁶ yet Elijah was sent to none of them except to a widow at Zarephath in Sidon. ²⁷ There were also many lepers in Israel in the time of the prophet Elisha, and none of them was cleansed except Naaman the Syrian." ²⁸ When they heard this, all in the synagogue were filled with rage. ²⁹ They got up, drove him out of the town, and led him to the brow of the hill on which their town was built, so that they might hurl him off the cliff. ³⁰ But he passed through the midst of them and went on his way.

This story fascinates me. The drama expresses many passionate emotions that I find deeply compelling to reflect upon—Jesus' self-disclosure expressed with great conviction and intentionality, community amazement that is both supportive and sneering, heated debates and pushback, angry recriminations and physical threats, and Jesus' calm determination to move forward. What exactly is going on here?!

Part of a larger synoptic thread (Matt 13:53–58, and Mark 6:1–6a), Luke's version adds more detail about the community's conflicts with Jesus (25–27),[7] including the physical threats to harm him (29). Most interesting to me as a queer person, though, is his citing of the messianic reference (Isaiah 61:1–2, and Isaiah 58:6) in verses 18–19. Luke is the only gospel with this story, which makes it stand out to me as significant. From a queer reading of this text I understand this as a disclosure, a coming out. Additionally, in response to my queer reading of the text, Brigitte Kahl suggests the presence of a two-step coming-out process in this story, where Jesus first proclaims the good news to the poor and is graciously received, and then continues his proclamation about the good news also being given to gentile communities that provokes great anger from the crowd.[8] Most significantly in my mind for this queer reading, the disclosure occurs within the larger story of Jesus' return home and his rejection by the community. I suspect that many queer persons can relate to the complexities and nuances of this type of experience, and so I am using it as a perspective to focus my engagement with the Nazareth story.

What are scholars saying? Scripture scholars view the Rejection at Nazareth text as an important statement by the Lukan author that intentionally introduces Jesus' mission and purpose to preach the gospel, the good news of God's salvific action in the community of Israel and beyond to the larger gentile community. It emphasizes Jesus' Spirit-led, prophetic ministry and describes the themes present in the remainder of the gospel. Mullins states, "Placing it [the story] here gives Jesus the opportunity to make his programmatic statement about his ministry and serves as the starting point from which he sets out on his great missionary itinerary, the final phase of which brings him to Jerusalem."[9]

Luke Timothy Johnson, emphasizing the prophetic nature of the text, understands the passage to be a "programmatic prophecy" that intends to focus an understanding of the gospel narrative. The Isaiah reference in the passage serves to describe the character of Jesus' ministry as prophetic:

7. Brigitte Kahl notes about these conflicts that the Lukan author is the only gospel writer to add the widow of Zarephath and Naaman the Syrian, both of whom were marginalized as "the ultimate other-than-us." Personal correspondence to me, October 21, 2017.

8. Kahl makes the point that Jesus might have been tempted to disclose only the truth-telling that was popular in the community, but "he has to tell the *whole* truth." Personal correspondence to me, October 21, 2017.

9. Mullins, *Gospel of Luke*, 168.

"The radical character of this mission is specified above all by its being offered to and accepted by those who were outcasts of the people."[10] What is the intention of the rejection themes in the narrative? For Johnson, Jesus' "intimation" to the community is that,

> the prophet would be for all and not just them—and in the reader's understanding, that God's visitation and salvation were to be for the poor and oppressed of all nations and not just for the Jews—that arouses the neighbor's wrath, impelling them to fulfill Jesus' statement: he is not acceptable in his own country because his mission extends beyond his own country. Luke thus provides the last part of the prophetic pattern that of rejection by the people.[11]

In this interpretation, the intention and placement of the story in the Lukan narrative defines God's desire to care for the marginalized and outcast as the fundamental focus of Jesus' mission for all peoples. For Johnson, the Isaiah reference "also serves as a programmatic statement of Jesus' prophetic word"[12] that challenges systems of power that disenfranchise.

In an understanding of the larger context of the Luke-Acts narrative, feminist analysis takes a more critical and diverse view, seeing in the entire work an ambiguous combination of female empowerment and patriarchal control. Amy-Jill Levine notes "Some readers have found and will continue to find in the Third Gospel the summons to liberation; others will find numerous barriers to that same goal."[13] Placing Luke within the context of the strong presence of the Roman Empire, Brigitte Kahl sees in the self-contradictory narratives a "hermeneutics of conspiracy"[14] whereby the texts are filled with coded language and countercultural intent that was a necessary aspect of the author's negotiation with imperial power. Rather than engage in either ignoring the patriarchal aspects of the texts or restricting an analysis to critique of those patriarchal aspects, she seeks a "third way" whereby the contradictory voices can be examined, and their significance understood. This "reading Luke against Luke" can provide a scripturally based countercultural reading.[15] She states,

---

10. Johnson, *Gospel of Luke*, 81.

11. Johnson, *Gospel of Luke*, 82.

12. Johnson, *Prophetic Jesus, Prophetic Church*, 79.

13. Levine, "Introduction," in *A Feminist Companion to Luke*, 2.

14. Kahl, "Reading Luke Against Luke," 72.

15. Kahl, "Reading Luke Against Luke," 87–88.

> For the most remarkable thing about Luke is that next to the com-
> promise he seeks, or possibly had to achieve with the 'upper levels'
> of the *imperium romanum,* he provides, in the first chapter of his
> story of the beginning, something like a set of directions for an
> opposite reading of the text, from the perspective of an egalitarian,
> horizontal 'below.'[16]

For Kahl, based on the structure of the text itself, the Lukan narrative can
be read with an intent to discover the meaning from the perspective of the
socially disempowered and marginalized.

Engaging postcolonial analysis of the full Luke-Acts narrative, Virginia Burrus views it as "notably preoccupied with power, pulsing with
the energy of charged exchanges between centre and periphery—rich and
poor, urban and rural, Jew and Gentile, the Jerusalem temple and the land
of Israel, Rome and those subjugated under imperial rule."[17] The power dynamic places Jesus within the context of Roman and Judean politics, which
Luke uses to both create an apologetics for the Roman Empire and, at the
same time, critique it from the perspective of the reign of God. Burrus understands this to be a strategy of resistance to imperial authority, creating a
powerful, but subtle, critique:

> . . . it should not be denied that Luke-Acts carries a message of
> political subversion. The subversiveness of the text may be less,
> however, in the extent to which it opposes the totalizing claims of
> one empire—the Roman—with the totalizing claims of another—
> God's Kingdom—than the very ambivalence that has earned Luke
> his reputation as an apologist for Rome. . . . Luke has, in the act of
> laying claim to the political values of Rome, used those same values
> to interrogate the oppressive policies of empire, thereby wedging
> open room within which a persecuted people might manoeuvre.[18]

For Burrus, then, Luke-Acts can be seen as a text challenging imperializing
and universalizing contexts with a powerful resistance.

Explicitly queer readings of the Gospel of Luke also highlight the
transgressive and destabilizing character of the narrative as a result of Jesus'
prophetic power. For Robert E. Goss, the Lukan Jesus is queer in that he
"destabilizes the symbolic world, turning it inside-out and transgressing

16. Kahl, "Reading Luke Against Luke," 86.

17. Burrus, "Luke-Acts," 133.

18. Burrus, "Luke-Acts," 139.

social boundaries to create a queer utopia, the reign of God."[19] He reads Luke with the hope that "Jesus the queer prophet will inspire twenty-first-century Christianity to embrace the gendered and sexually different, the broken-bodied, and the marginalized."[20]

Other gospel stories refer to Jesus and coming out and its relation to queer lives. Thomas Bohache, reflecting upon Luke's story of Jesus' baptism in the Gospel of Matthew, views baptism as symbolizing coming out, a process where we "finally come to terms with who we are and seek to shed the homophobia that has accrued in our psyches during the formative years."[21] For Marcella Althaus-Reid, the temptation narratives in Mark's Gospel show Jesus as engaging in a coming-out process. She states, "The queer man of God came out and somehow conquered; he conquered hearts and his community was becoming strong enough to present a different or alternative lifestyle."[22] For Robert E. Goss, in the Gospel of John, the theme of coming out "enables queer folk to appreciate God's coming out in Jesus and the struggle engendered in the narrative. God's coming out in Jesus resonates with queer life experiences."[23]

From this brief overview of scholarship related to both the Nazareth text and the larger Gospel of Luke, we can find important ideas to support a queer reading of Jesus' return to his home community. The Jesus depicted in Luke, who queers established power structures to make space for the inclusion of those whom society considers to be outcast, speaks a word of freedom and acceptance to LGBTQI persons. There is space in the text for subversive readings that challenge social discourses of power that restrict human freedom and suggest transgressive possibilities to support queer empowerment.

While the story is about introducing Jesus' Spirit-led mission from the perspective of a queer reading, it seems to capture the dynamic rhythm of a coming-out experience. Coming to clarity about one's gender and sexual identification is often an experience of truth-telling that occurs over time with many revelations along the way. Before Jesus can speak to his community with conviction, he first goes to be baptized by John, where his Spirit-led ministry is authorized. In that process, his identity is

19. Goss, "Luke," 526.
20. Goss, "Luke," 526.
21. Bohache, "Matthew," 499.
22. Althaus-Reid, "Mark," 523.
23. Goss, "John," 549.

affirmed spiritually. He then goes alone to the desert to engage with God more deeply, to reflect upon and to understand more fully his ministry and identity. With a sense of conviction and intentionality from those experiences, he reveals his truth-telling to his home community, and it shocks them with amazement and arouses their anger. In the end, they cannot accept him and reject him with force and threat to his body. But he moves on from them to live his life and engage his ministry away from those who cannot accept him.

What might it mean for queer lives? For me, there is a familiarity about the dynamic represented in the story. I offer an interpretation of it as an example of one possible coming-out journey, rather than making that interpretation prescriptive for all coming-out experiences.

In many queer lives, the coming-out process has numerous steps along the way. Seeking to know a sense of authenticity in our deepest becoming-selfhood-in-relation, some find it through a connection with a transcendent power or God. A fragile embracing of a more authentic becoming-selfhood-in-relation becomes firmer and assured in our efforts to understand ourselves in different circumstances and contexts. Maybe the location is a nightclub, or a bar to drink with others, or a softball team or a political advocacy group where one lives openly in an identification of becoming-selfhood-in-relation that is counter to social norms. From these positions of strength and cohesion, however modest or firm, the risk is taken to come out in our world (family, culture, religious tradition, community), often when one has the emotional resources and supports to face the possibility of rejection. For some there is, increasingly, acceptance. For many the acceptance will come through a long and challenging process of dialogue with those in our world. For some that acceptance will never come and the risk of attempting it is too great. At other times, circumstances beyond our control can force a revelation of our becoming-selfhood-in-relation at a time not of our choosing. Each instance presents a possibility to engage with the reactions of those who are members of the community, especially ones that affect us most personally. The threat of violence is an ever-present reality that queer persons, especially transgender persons, face. Being open requires protection from those threats. It also requires courageous truth-telling. Like Jesus, queer persons often make the decision to move forward away from, but still engaged with, the very communities that have nurtured us in order to live more truthful and integrated lives.

As I stated earlier, I bring the following questions to the Lukan text: What can queer persons learn and understand about their lives from this story? Can it support coming out? From this theological reflection and queer reading I propose several insights that might support and sustain a coming-out process.

First, I read this text as a challenging example of a fundamental experience of queer coming out: *the truth-telling of coming out is relational;* queer truth-telling about our lives occurs in communities that accept us, as well as in ones that cannot accept queer lives. Each context challenges us to engage in the hard work of truth-telling, negotiating its effects in relation to the diverse social identities of queer lives. When we come out we need to be prepared to engage openly and, at the same time, protect ourselves from that which can undermine the freedom we gain from embracing a more authentic becoming-selfhood-in-relation.

Second, *coming out is not neutral;* it is an embodied social and political empowerment that is often filled with risk. In fact, you might say that it comes with a warning label. Jesus' truth-telling in the text subjects him to rejection from the community where he has roots. Acceptance goes a long way in helping to make the risk of openness manageable. However, the reality of rejection is a necessary partner in the act of truth-telling that places us in opposition to social and cultural norms. Truthful openness, acceptance, and rejection become the tools that construct the stability and instability of the coming-out process. Learning to embrace both the positive experiences of affirmation and the negative experiences of rejection are ways to develop and articulate a sense of personal integrity.

Third, *coming out encompasses experiences of disruption and instability, as well as stability and coherence.* The text vividly depicts Jesus' truthful declaration, his coming out, as something that is simultaneously a coherent articulation of selfhood and ministerial intent, and deeply disruptive to the community's expectations. From a queer perspective, one might understand how great a risk Jesus took in that revealing. The conflict that ensued between Jesus and the community forced Jesus to defend himself from their dismissal of his truth-telling about himself and his ministry. His pushback reveals his conviction about his truth-telling. He has a clear sense of who he is and what he needs to accomplish. The way he chose to protect himself from their rage—passing through them and walking on to the next town—models a sense of when it is appropriate to let go and move forward. If the community cannot accept his truth, then he will need to move among others who will. The power of the experience of openness was both a sense of steadfastness about his understanding of truth and a flexibility to let go and allow a change to happen. The power of coming out, then, can be both the power of conviction and the power of change, both in individuals and communities. In its articulation of grounded conviction and the flexibility to change, this text provides LGBTQI persons with useful guides for living the reality of negotiating our self-revelations.

Finally, *coming out can lead to a greater sense of meaning and purpose for the work of justice*. The Lukan author connects the introduction of Jesus' prophetic, Spirit-led ministry to those whom society considers outcast to a larger task of proclaiming the justice and peace of the *basileia* of God. For queer lives coming out is a beginning of a journey, not an end. The authenticity and truthful living sought through coming out is connected to larger questions of how our empowered selves, our queer bodies, will work to create a more just world. The empowerment to one's becoming-selfhood-in-relation as a result of truth-telling, then, is not for self-actualization or personal fulfillment. Rather, its power is political in its intent to support the creation of a more just and inclusive community and world for those who are marginalized and penalized for their difference from normative culture. The truth-telling of coming out empowers the work of justice as right-relation and inclusive fairness.

Concluding Thoughts

Up to this point I have engaged in reflection on aspects of coming out that suggest the usefulness, even necessity, of engaging in a renewed theological discussion about the experience in queer lives. The first chapter focused its analysis on a personal experience of negotiating the fluidity and nuances of coming out and truth-telling within a family context full of intersectional realities and multiple needs. The second chapter presented a theological reflection using a biblical text that explored a positive interpretation of coming out as truth-telling, grounding it in Jesus' own truth-telling about his mission. Taken together, these chapters present a rationale for the task of reimagining coming out as a relational action, rather than as an essentialized identity declaration.

The next chapters move to the more constructive elements of my proposal. They seek to develop the themes of conscience formation and the practice of discernment as building blocks to support the notion of coming out as the erotic ethical practice of truth-telling. In naming coming out from this perspective as "disruptive coherence," I am signaling that the motion of change and the cohesion of identification work together to resist the creation of an essentialist identity. These ideas come into focus more clearly after first developing with sufficient clarity the meaning of erotic ethical practice as a way to consider the process of coming out, which is the subject of the next chapter.

3

Toward Erotic Ethical Practice

Somewhere, on the edge of consciousness, there is what I call *a mythical norm*, which each one of us within our hearts knows "that is not me." In america, this norm is usually defined as white, thin, male, young, heterosexual, christian, and financially secure. It is within this mythical norm that the trappings of power reside within this society.

—AUDRE LORDE, *SISTER OUTSIDER*[1]

Over thirty years ago, Audre Lorde used the concept of "a mythical norm" to articulate her critique of the categories that society considered to be normal that excluded her. She stated, "As a forty-nine-year-old Black lesbian feminist socialist mother of two, including one boy, and a member of an interracial couple, I usually find myself a part of some group defined as other, deviant, inferior, or just plain wrong."[2] In the context of the time in which she was writing, she was challenging any attempt to homogenize real differences of experience that arise from specific social locations in relation to power. She was arguing for a feminism that took seriously the differences that race, class, and other indicators of social identity revealed.

With the development of postmodernist and post-structuralist theories, as well as queer studies, we would likely define what is mythically normative in a different way than Lorde did at that moment. We would highlight, for example, a larger diversity of categories of difference, their cultural constructions, and how these categories are fluid, with blurred boundaries and destabilized meanings. With this awareness, we can say that in the lived experience of many queer persons the process of coming out represents a way to defy any expression of "a mythical norm" and seeks

1. Lorde, *Sister Outsider*, 116.
2. Lorde, *Sister Outsider*, 114.

to articulate in the face of "that is not me" the reality of "that is me"—in its movements of ambiguity and incompleteness.

Queer studies and gender theories have helped us to see that there can be a problem with the idea of "that is me." If that "me" is understood as locked-in, individualized, and removed from interdependent relationships in the social world, then there is something false and inauthentic about that "self." What we understand to be "me" develops from a complex mix of discourses of culture, social institutions, power relations, and personal experiences that shape and form us. We are social beings for whom our inner selfhood emerges in relationship to transcendence, to God. In that dialogue with God, we come to understand over time and in our experiences a way of living in the world that feels real. Rather than the personal revelation of a "true self" that has existed in hiddenness, the action of coming out tells the truth about an important—but not singular or monolithic—aspect of a person that has been developed and revealed from our interaction in diverse communities and experiences. We articulate our becoming-self-hood-in-the-world in a profound way that has the capacity to develop as we grow and change. In addition, we articulate our becoming-selfhood-in-the-world within an intersectional social context in which we simultaneously exist in several social worlds that engage power in different ways.

This chapter sets the intellectual context of this project in the literature of queer theory, queer theology, and an understanding of the practices of communities. I do not seek to engage fully the complex and diverse literature in each area. Instead, I look selectively to ask specific questions that will be necessary for my argument: What do these literatures say specifically about coming out? How might it be useful in creating new understandings about the process of coming out that is disconnected from a declaration of essentialized identity? In focusing attention on how these literatures speak about (or are related to) the process of coming out, it seeks to establish a rationale for understanding coming out as an ethical practice. When we embrace both the theoretical critiques of queer theory *and* queer theology's praxis in lived Christian experience, it creates an opportunity to consider a different conversation about coming out. When rooted in ethics and the practices of religious communities, the energy of coming out resides in the truth-telling that disrupts established understandings. In this disruption resides the potential to create more diverse communities that have the capacity to embrace gender and sexual difference.

Queer Theory: Coming Out Is Not a Meaningful Category

Queer theory's critique of a traditional notion of coming out provides a necessary starting point to a reexamination of coming out. Its challenge to an essentialist understanding of identity responds to a significant aspect of queer lived experience—that the boundaries of race, class, gender, sexuality, disability, religion (to name some key categories) are socially constructed, indistinct, and unsettled realities. Many people embrace multiple identifications and experience them in fluid and contingent ways. For queer theorists, coming out represents a misleading notion that does not consider the complexity of queer lives and is, therefore, not a useful or even accurate way to talk about sexuality and gender.

Critique: Sexuality Is a Socially Constructed Discourse of Power-Knowledge

In *The History of Sexuality, Volume 1*, Michel Foucault challenged the idea of an inherent, true sexual identity; rather, he argued that sexuality is an historical construct produced as a way to control sex and sexual desires. Discourses about sexuality, developed through instruments and techniques of social and cultural power, regulate the normative definitions of sex, bodies, and pleasure that society holds to be appropriate. He focuses on the "repression hypothesis"—a belief that open discussions of sex were socially repressed in modern industrial societies—and expresses doubt about its validity. He posits that, in fact, there was a "discursive explosion" during that period in which the open discussion of sexuality was regulated to certain relationships, locations, and prescribed languages.[3] These sexual discourses—expressed in Christian laws, pastoral practice, and civil laws that were developed, starting in the Middle Ages, from the influences and practices of the Christian sacrament of penance[4]—focused on heterosexual monogamy and set apart categories of sexuality considered to be unnatural. Earlier in Christian history, actions of sodomy were condemned as aberrant and treated through law, but it was nineteenth-century medicalized constructions of sexuality that created the identity of homosexual. Sex changed from an act to a sense of one's being, nature, or essence.[5] The

3. Foucault, *History of Sexuality, Volume 1*, 10–18.

4. Foucault, *History of Sexuality, Volume 1*, 18–23, 58–59.

5. Foucault, *History of Sexuality, Volume 1*, 37–44. Foucault states on page 43, "The sodomite had been a temporary aberration; the homosexual was now a species."

resulting development of a scientific study of sexuality (*Sciencia Sexualis*) sought to produce the "truth of sex" and maintain it through social control and instruments of power, particularly through the practice of *confession*.[6] For Foucault, "sexuality" and its "truth" were invented as discourses to regulate sex.[7] Discursive practices related to sex construct sexuality, and this sexual discourse develops and regulates what is considered normal and abnormal. For Foucault, because sex is a function of the discourse of "sexuality," the way to "counterattack" against its controls is to embrace "bodies and pleasures," rather than "sex-desire."[8]

If sexual identity is not an essence and not "natural" to one's being, and hetero/homosexual are constructed categories, then coming out, as the revelation of a hidden true nature, becomes a meaningless conversation that a normalizing and disciplining sexuality discourse imposes. Foucault challenges the notion that sexual desire expresses a truth about self-understanding, stating,

> And so, in this "question" of sex (in both senses: as interrogation and problematization, and as the need for confession and integration into a field of rationality), two processes emerge, the one always conditioning the other: we demand that sex speaks the truth . . . and we demand that it tell us our truth, or rather, the deeply buried truth of that truth about ourselves which we think we possess in our immediate consciousness. We tell it its truth by deciphering what it tells us about that truth; it tells us our own by delivering up that part of it that escaped us. . . . Not, however, by reason of some natural property inherent in sex itself, but by virtue of the tactics of power immanent in this discourse.[9]

If the truth of the "self" in relation to sexuality is imposed through power-knowledge that exists in the discourse about sex, then the identity statement of coming out represents an uncritical acceptance of this imposition.

6. Foucault, *History of Sexuality, Volume 1*, 67–69.

7. I realize that there might be a tension between my proposal to understand coming out as a practice of truth-telling and Foucault's stance that sexuality is a discourse created through required truth-telling of sexual sins. Because I understand truth-telling to be an ethical action of responsible freedom, rather than an admission of guilt or shame for sin, my proposal counters this idea in Foucault. In this way my thinking is closer to a later period of Foucault and his work on *parrhesia* ("truthful speaking"). See chapter 6 for a more detailed discussion.

8. Foucault, *History of Sexuality, Volume 1*, 157.

9. Foucault, *History of Sexuality, Volume 1*, 69–70.

Critique: Sexuality Presents False Binaries and Incoherent Definitions

Deeply influenced by Foucault's analysis of the social construction of sexuality, in *Epistemology of the Closet,* Eve Kosofsky Sedgwick challenged the idea of the closet as a simplistic in/out binary of public/private, secrecy/disclosure of sexual identity. In fact, there is a fluid movement between these experiences of in/out in various contexts and situations over time such that images of coming out "regularly interfaces" with images of the closet.[10] She argued that to understand modern Western culture, one must critically examine the homosexual/heterosexual binary, which is deeply ingrained with the fluid movement related to the experience of the closet.

Sedgwick questioned the "radical and irreducible incoherence" of homo/heterosexual definitions, which exists in discourses of homosexuality. These conflicting discourses indicate both a "minoritizing" understanding of homosexuality that views it as an essentialist, fixed identity for a small group of persons, and a "universalizing" understanding that views a spectrum of fluid and destabilized erotic sensibilities and practices.[11] Since the identity of homosexuality is a confused and contested reality, she proposes "a study of the incoherent dispensation itself" that would disrupt the minoritizing/universalizing "impasse" completely.[12] The closet holds no meaning when the minoritizing view is disrupted because a destabilized notion of sexual identity holds the capacity of experiencing variable sexual desires. Within a construct of fluid sexual identities, then, coming out holds no significance.

Critique: There Is No Essence of Gender; Gender Is Performed

Judith Butler built upon Foucault's theory with an analysis of the social construction of gender. In *Gender Trouble: Feminism and the Subversion of Identity,* she argued that gender and sexuality, rather than being expressions of an innate identity, are learned and repeated expressions of a culture's understanding—that is, gender is not an essence of self, rather, it is imitation, enacted from socially constructed ideas about gender and solidified

---

10. Sedgwick, *Epistemology of the Closet,* 71–72.

11. Sedgwick, *Epistemology of the Closet,* 1, 82–90.

12. Sedgwick, *Epistemology of the Closet,* 90.

through repeated acts of performance.[13] In the context of Butler's theory of gender performativity, coming out as a specific identity represents an essentialized notion of being lesbian or gay.

Butler interrogated the idea of coming out directly in "Imitation and Gender Subordination," stating, "I'm not at ease with 'lesbian theories, gay theories,' . . . identity categories tend to be instruments of regulatory regimes, whether as the normalizing categories of oppressive structures or as the rallying points for a liberatory contestation of that very oppression."[14] Specifically, she claimed that coming out produces "a new and different closet," that is,

> being "out" always depends to some extent on being "in," it gains meaning only within that polarity. Hence being "out" must produce the closet again and again in order to maintain itself as "out." In this sense *outness* can only produce a new opacity, and *the closet* produces the promise of a disclosure that can, by definition, never come.[15]

Butler understands that "gender is a kind of imitation for which there is no original"[16] and this understanding allows for subverting, resisting, and destabilizing the categories of gender and sexual identity. This subversion prevents the act of naming one's identity from becoming a new and different closet. Coming out, then, can be appropriately used as a "strategic provisionality"—not a "strategic essentialism"—that can be a site of "contest and revision" of that identity.[17]

13. Butler, *Gender Trouble*. See on page 136, "In other words, acts, gestures, and desire produce the effect of an internal core or substance, but produce this *on the surface* of the body, through the play of signifying absences that suggest, but never reveal, the organizing principle of identity as a cause. Such acts, gestures, enactments, generally constructed, are *performative* in the sense that the essence or identity that they otherwise purport to express are *fabrications* manufactured and sustained through corporeal signs and other discursive means. That the gendered body is performative suggests that it has no ontological status apart from the various acts which constitute its reality. . . . If the inner truth of gender is a fabrication and if a true gender is a fantasy instituted and inscribed on the surface of bodies, then it seems that genders can be neither true nor false, but are only produced as the truth effects of a discourse of primary and stable identity." Also, see on page 140, "Gender ought not be construed as a stable identity or locus of agency from which various acts follow; rather, gender is an identity tenuously constructed in time, instituted in an exterior space through a *stylized repetition of acts*."

14. Butler, "Imitation and Gender Insubordination," 308.

15. Butler, "Imitation and Gender Insubordination," 309.

16. Butler, "Imitation and Gender Insubordination," 313.

17. Butler, "Imitation and Gender Insubordination," 312.

Critique: Coming Out Is an Act of Freedom and Resistance, Not Liberation

David Halperin ties his discussion about coming out to Foucault's notion that power is a reality that is constitutive of any social relations.[18] Power does not exist as *only* the domination of one group with power over another that is disempowered. Rather, power characterizes "relations of ongoing struggle"—*both domination and resistance*—between groups and individuals in society. For Halperin, a focus on queer liberation obscures the acts of resistance that are embedded in these relations of power. Resistance, then, is the goal of oppositional sexual politics, stating *"The aim of oppositional politics is therefore not liberation but resistance."*[19]

From this perspective, Halperin views the closet as "the product of complex relations of power," and thus coming out as an opportunity to alter the power dynamics in a struggle with socially imposed sexual normativity. He states,

> If to come out is to release oneself from the state of unfreedom, that is not because coming out constitutes an escape from the reach of power to a place outside of power; rather, coming out puts into play a different set of power relations and alters the dynamics of personal and political struggle. *Coming out is an act of freedom, then, not in the sense of liberation but in the sense of resistance.*[20]

From this perspective, coming out is a personal and political action of resistance against socially imposed heteronormative discourses, rather than a liberation from a false "self."

Queer Theology: Queer Experiences and Religious Traditions in Conversation

Queer theorists provide an important critique and challenge to the idea that sexual identity is an essence of "self," fixed and immutable, that, after being hidden, is embraced in a coming-out experience. Queer theology, influenced by this philosophical perspective, wrestles with these critiques of

18. Halperin, *Saint Foucault*, 16–18.
19. Halperin, *Saint Foucault*, 18.
20. Halperin, *Saint Foucault*, 29–30.

essentialism as it searches for ways to discuss queer experiences, including the process of coming out, from the perspective of Christian theology.

In *Gay and Lesbian Theologies: Repetitions with Critical Difference*, Elizabeth Stuart charts the development of gay and lesbian theologies from beginnings in the 1970s through the 1990s. She makes a convincing case that an uncritical acceptance of the modernist notions of a static, individualized self, combined with the failure of identity-based theologies to respond adequately to the AIDS crisis, revealed the weakness and inadequacies of existing gay and lesbian theologies (liberal, liberationist, lesbian feminist).[21] In contrast, queer theology embraces queer theorists' belief that the goal is not to come out—in the sense of revealing a hidden sexual and gender identity that is an essence of "self"—but "to liberate everyone from contemporary constructions of sexuality (Foucault) and gender (Butler)."[22] Therefore, since it is not an identity-based theology, queer theology deconstructs gender and sexual identities, but it does so through an understanding of our "baptismal incorporation to the body of Christ."[23] Further, queer theology posits the inherent and historical queerness of Christianity (especially seen in constructions of the body of Jesus and the Trinity), and rejects a notion of metanarratives to explain humans and their actions in history.[24] Queer theology, then, combines postmodernist standpoints with the Christian theological and scriptural traditions to examine the intricacies of LGBTQI lives. In this way, queer theology roots itself firmly in recognizably religious discourses. Stuart states,

> Queer theology, though it usually begins with issues of sexuality, is not really 'about' sexuality in the way that gay and lesbian theology is about sexuality. Queer theology is actually about theology. In gay and lesbian theology sexuality interrogated theology; in queer theology, theology interrogates sexuality but from a different place than modern theology has done, the place of tradition. Queer theology denies the 'truth' of sexuality and hence declares that it is not stable enough to build a theology upon.[25]

Thus, in its acceptance of the deconstruction of the modern notion of a self, queer theology rejects sexual and gender identity as a basis of theology and

21. Stuart, *Gay and Lesbian Theologies*.
22. Stuart, *Gay and Lesbian Theologies*, 89.
23. Stuart, *Gay and Lesbian Theologies*, 102.
24. Stuart, *Gay and Lesbian Theologies*, 102
25. Stuart, *Gay and Lesbian Theologies*, 102–3.

reclaims Christian theological and scriptural traditions as an authority in conversation with queer lives.

Before I move on to continue the discussion of queer theology and its understandings of coming out, it is important to note several texts from the period of gay and lesbian theology and gay liberation theology (as Stuart defines it), that, although grounded in more identity-based understandings of coming out and its limitations, provide important insights about coming out as a transformative practice. I will mention them briefly to highlight some of their contributions.

Chris Glaser's *Coming Out as Sacrament*, understands coming out as a "a rite of vulnerability that reveals the sacred in our lives."[26] For him, coming out relates closely to the Christian sacrament of Communion: "both involve a sacrifice and an offering that creates at-one-ment or communion with God and with others."[27] In *Coming Out Within: Stages of Spiritual Awakening for Lesbians and Gay Men*, Craig O'Neill and Kathleen Ritter examine gay and lesbian experiences of loss and their stages of transformation as a spiritual awakening that creates wholeness and integrity.[28] In *Gay Theology Without Apology*, Gary David Comstock develops a personal theological and ministerial stance that "examines the Bible and Christianity not with the purpose of fitting in or finding a place in them, but fitting them into and changing them according to the particular experiences of lesbian/bisexual/gay people."[29] The decision to come out for him was not from an examination of church doctrine or Scriptures; rather, his experience of being a "closeted student pastor" helped him to understand his responsibility to the lesbian and gay persons of his parish and his desire to be available to minister to them in their struggle.[30] Finally, in *Know My Name: A Gay Liberation Theology*, Richard Cleaver understands coming out in the struggle of gay and lesbian persons to name themselves and that which oppresses them: "We must name ourselves and name our oppression. Naming is how scripture represents people as claiming their own lives and power."[31] Naming oppression

26. Glaser, *Coming Out as Sacrament*, 9.

27. Glaser, *Coming Out as Sacrament*, 15.

28. O'Neill and Ritter, *Coming Out Within*.

29. Comstock, *Gay Theology Without Apology*, 4.

30. Comstock, *Gay Theology Without Apology*, 25–26.

31. Cleaver, *Know My Name*, 58.

occurs through struggling with it; in naming themselves gay and lesbian, persons are better able to hear God's call.[32]

Returning now to an overview of queer theology texts and coming out, a few theologians—not all of whom would identify themselves as queer theologians—have examined coming out from varying theological perspectives that seek to move beyond essentialist identity disclosure. With this brief overview of each work, I hope to provide important groundwork for the task of reimagining ways to think about coming out.

In *Faith Beyond Resentment: Fragments Catholic and Gay,* James Alison speaks about coming out in the language of "finding a story."[33] For Alison, God invites us to "inscribe ourselves" in the biblical story, thereby finding our own stories. He states,

> My conviction is that there is only one Bible story, and that it is the story told by God, and it is within this that we are invited to inscribe ourselves. In other words, God calls us into being through giving us the gift of story, and that uncompleted story is one in harmony with, and nourished by, the fragments of biblical nudges towards it.[34]

The story that we are called to "inhabit" does not entail a reaction against something pushing against us negatively, but rather, embracing and rejoicing in that movement of becoming more fully human and connected to God's call to embrace the story of our lives as we understand it in relation with God's story.

A significant element of the development of our story is inscribed in God's story, is the story we have of coming out. Alison rejects simplistic narratives of coming out as a once-and-for-all gay actualization into an idealized "self." Rather, he looks at coming out as a process of moving toward greater truthfulness and humanness that grounds a person in a moral stance of penitence and courage:

> Wherever a coming-out story is real, it also includes what I would call a penitential element: how I was a coward and failed to stand up for my brothers when the heat was on, but am now being given the grace to stand up and risk opprobrium . . . The real drama of the coming-out experience is precisely that it is the beginning of a taking of positions . . . and the discovery that by taking position I

32. Cleaver, *Know My Name,* 58–61.

33. Alison, *Faith Beyond Resentment,* 194–208.

34. Alison, *Faith Beyond Resentment,* 196–97.

become not 'a gay man,' whatever that might be, but a real partici-
pant in the life of the human race . . . But it is also the realization
that my previous failure to stand up for the weak was not simply
neutral, but left me in collusion with violence.[35]

For Alison, the power of coming out lies not in the disclosure of a sexual
identity, but in one's embrace of a greater humanness that makes possible
an awareness of the ways in which we have not fully supported those
who are vulnerable. Theologically connecting penitence to creation, he
views the new creation of coming out as the power of bold truth-telling.
When we find our story inscribed in God's story, we can "speak out of an
unanswerable boldness . . . not in reaction to the authorities, but simply
truth coming into being."[36]

In his contribution to the anthology, *Queer Theology: Rethinking the
Western Body*, Eugene F. Rogers Jr. places the work of a queer theorist in conversation with traditional Christian theology. In "Bodies Demand Language:
Thomas Aquinas," he examines the claim—clearly articulated in the chapter
title—which he believes is common to both Judith Butler and Thomas Aquinas, "that a body is that which demands language."[37] He challenges the idea
that natural law functions primarily for Aquinas as a way to articulate moral
stances, noting that appeals to virtue are most common. His analysis of the
two exceptions to this claim, i.e., truth-telling and same-gender relations,
or in his words, "lying and lying with a member of the same sex," disrupts
traditional interpretations of natural law in Aquinas.[38] Through his queering
of Thomistic theology he articulates "an exhortation to come out, to obey
the 'natural' demand of the body for language."[39]

Rogers examines the construction of natural law in Aquinas's *Summa Theologiae* and the *Commentary on Romans* and sees that for Aquinas
it is not a category that primarily defines his thinking; rather, Aquinas
articulates moral claims most frequently in the language of virtue. There
are two exceptions where Aquinas seems to appeal to natural law and not
virtue: lying and homosexuality. Basing his critique on the virtues of justice and gratitude, Aquinas views homosexuality as "God's punishment

35. Alison, *Faith Beyond Resentment,* 200–201.
36. Alison, *Faith Beyond Resentment,* 205.
37. Rogers, "Bodies Demand Language," 176–87.
38. Rogers, "Bodies Demand Language," 176.
39. Rogers, "Bodies Demand Language," 176.

for Gentile injustice and idolatry" that prevents them from seeing what is true. According to Rogers,

> Liberation theologians can now appeal to Thomas Aquinas to claim that human beings cannot reach correct intellectual conclusions under unjust conditions. Rather, injustice leads human beings to mistake the truth about what is natural . . . homosexuality does not originate as an independent sin, but as punishment for *previous* sins of social injustice.[40]

Rogers sees this as a complicating debate about natural law because in this interpretation, principles of natural law are subordinate to principles of virtue.

This interpretation presents a less essentialist understanding of natural law—habits of virtue, which are performative, are how we recognize moral laws. These habits are human beings' participation in God's performance:

> natural law is the this-worldly performance of God's prudence, God's prudence in act. As we participate in God's prudence, natural law is no *independent, totalizing* source of knowledge, but part of a changing mix. The natures in question are defined not Platonically as essences off in some ideal space, but Aristotelianly as *internal* principles of *change*.[41]

Further, these natures are elements of something internal that empowers humans and are dynamically alive with change and movement. We know these principles through our performance of the practices of virtue.

He then moves specifically to examining the two exceptions where Aquinas appeals to the natural law, rather than habits of virtue: lying and homosexuality. Rogers states that Aquinas understands a lie to be that which is opposed to the truth and that contradicts what the rational mind understands to be true. It is the nature of the mind to understand truth, and a lie is counter to this truth. Similarly, a sin against nature contradicts what the body understands to be true. Rogers sees that, for Aquinas, truth-telling applies to both speech and bodies in a specific sense: "lies of the genitals resemble lies of the tongue because both are better described as acts of the whole person; actions of tongue or genitals can both make the whole person a liar."[42] According to Rogers, this belief led Aquinas to condemn

40. Rogers, "Bodies Demand Language," 179.
41. Rogers, "Bodies Demand Language," 180.
42. Rogers, "Bodies Demand Language," 182.

homosexuality as a sin against nature. However, for Rogers, from a contemporary perspective it could be interpreted as an exhortation to come out.

> Homosexuality, one infers, is for Thomas in some respects a lie of the body. We might today adopt the similar reasoning to an opposite conclusion: heterosexual activity by gay and lesbian people is exposed when their bodies give them the lie, and coming out is the bringing into community, the semiotic offering, of the body's truth telling.[43]

This truth-telling is about self-definition that is formed and embraced within a community in which we interpret ourselves and make sense of the truth we see in ourselves. Rogers concludes that coming out is precisely the body's demand for language, and as language, an aspect of participation in human community. In his interpretation, coming out cannot be viewed as an individualized self-disclosure of a hidden essence.

Patrick S. Cheng relates the process of coming out very specifically to the classical Christian theological doctrine of revelation—human knowledge of God, how we come to understand that knowledge, and what that knowledge tells us about the truth of God. In *Radical Love: An Introduction to Queer Theology*, Cheng understands God's revelation of Godself as coming out: "the doctrine of revelation can be understood as *God's coming out as radical love* . . . the doctrine of revelation parallels the self-disclosure that occurs when an LGBT person comes out to someone whom he or she loves about her or his sexuality and/or gender identity."[44] Further, God's coming out is a radical act of love that dissolves existing boundaries in three ways.[45] First, God's revelation—God's coming out—dissolves boundaries between the divine and human, making it possible for human limitation to engage transcendence. Second, God's revelation dissolves the boundaries between the powerful and the weak. This incarnational aspect of God reveals God's compassion for those who are marginalized and God's "preferential option" for the excluded. Third, God's revelation dissolves the boundaries of knowing and unknowing in that our knowledge of God "is always in a state of transformation and unknowing."[46]

In his work on queer Christology, *From Sin to Amazing Grace: Discovering the Queer Christ*, Cheng develops a model of the Queer Christ

43. Rogers, "Bodies Demand Language," 184.
44. Cheng, *Radical Love*, 45.
45. Cheng, *Radical Love*, 45–48.
46. Cheng, *Radical Love*, 48.

using coming out/revelation as an interpretive lens. His model of the "Out Christ" rests in the Christian belief that the true nature of God is revealed in the Christ event: "The Out Christ arises out of the understanding that God reveals Godself most fully in the person of Jesus Christ. In other words, God 'comes out of the closet' in the person of Jesus Christ . . . God comes out in the incarnation, ministry, crucifixion, and resurrection of Jesus Christ."[47] From this model of the Out Christ, he understands sin to be that which opposes our deeper connection to Christ and grace to be that which connects us more deeply to Christ. In the logic of his argument, then, sin can be understood as the closet—with its isolation, and corrosion of self-esteem and well-being—and grace as the capacity for coming out, that is, a disclosure of one's sexual and/or gender identity. Cheng sees the process of coming out as infused with God's grace:

> Regardless of how one ultimately comes out, the act of coming out reflects the very nature of a God who is also constantly coming out and revealing Godself to us in the Out Christ. Coming out is a gift that is accompanied by other gifts such as self-love, the love for others, the overcoming of shame and internalized homophobia. Coming out is not something that can be 'willed' or 'earned'; it can only happen as an act of grace from God.[48]

Importantly, Cheng notes that coming out necessarily takes many forms, and that for queer persons from communities of color, the intersectional dynamics of race and ethnicity with queerness takes on a significant complexity.[49] He believes that, "In the end, communities of color have their unique ways of dealing with the coming out issue, which can take the form of God's amazing grace."[50]

Moving outside of the Christian tradition, there are helpful discussions about coming out and religious connections as well. Scott Siraj al-Haqq Kugle articulates a perspective from Islam about coming out in the context of Muslim gay, lesbian, and transgender lived experience.[51] He

---

47. Cheng, *From Sin to Amazing Grace*, 81. This model is one of seven that Cheng develops in this work: The Erotic Christ, The Out Christ, The Liberator Christ, The Transgressive Christ, The Self-Loving Christ, The Interconnected Christ, The Hybrid Christ.

48. Cheng, *From Sin to Amazing Grace*, 87.

49. For further reading on this dynamic, see Monroe, "When and Where I Enter"; Griffin, *Their Own Receive Them Not*, 142–65; Lightsey, *Our Lives Matter*, 31–35.

50. Cheng, *From Sin to Amazing Grace*, 89.

51. Kugle, *Living Out Islam*.

states that for Muslims, subjective identity (including sexual orientation and gender identity) is formed from a complex engagement of individual psyche, family relationships, religious community, and national context. Thus, the movement for gay, lesbian, and transgender rights focuses on finding their place in the tradition, rather than on the dynamic of openness or hiddenness: "This movement is not about being 'out' as opposed to being 'in the closet.' Rather, it is about finding ways to live out one's Islam with dignity and integrity by reconciling one's sexuality and gender with one's faith."[52] He examines six "modes of activism" through which this reconciling action occurs: engaging religious tradition, challenging family and community, adapting religious politics, adjusting secular politics, forging minority alliances, journeying toward individual identity.[53]

From Jewish Scripture, Jay Michaelson takes seriously the ninth commandment—"Thou shalt not bear false witness"—when understanding coming out. For him, the religious injunction to live lives of honesty and integrity makes coming out a religious act.[54]

> The danger of dishonesty touches each of us who refuses, out of fear or love, to grapple with the difficult facts of what it means to be human. This is how I understand the name 'Israel,' given to Jacob after he wrestles with a man all night—that he is a God-wrestler, a truth-wrestler, someone who allows himself to be embraced, enveloped, even defeated by truth. His is a quintessentially religious story, and his is the challenge to which we must rise.[55]

Ultimately, for Michaelson, coming out provides the opportunity to live a life of integrity, which he views as a deeply religious act.

Continuing with the theme of living with integrity, in *Transgender Journeys*, Virginia Ramey Mollenkott and Vanessa Sheridan view coming out as transgender to be "an act of faith": "It is a compelling proclamation of God's love and acceptance for us as people. Coming out is a powerful declaration about our individual acceptance of that divine love as we, in turn, embody and share the love of God with others."[56] They see coming out as transgender as a way to live out lives of integrity, confident in God's love and acceptance.

52. Kugle, *Living Out Islam*, 2.
53. Kugle, *Living Out Islam*, 3–4.
54. Michaelson, *God vs. Gay?*
55. Michaelson, *God vs. Gay?* 46.
56. Mollenkott and Sheridan, *Transgender Journeys*, 139.

It is important to note that coming-out narratives for transgender persons can possess their own unique set of concerns that differentiate them from lesbian, gay, or bisexual coming-out narratives. Social scientist Lal Zimman argues that the complex dynamic of coming out before and after a change in gender role makes it imperative that transgender coming-out experiences be researched as a different genre of coming-out narrative. He states, "... transgender people experience coming out from two significantly different perspectives: before and after transitioning to the preferred gender role. The difference between these subjectivities must be examined before a full understanding of coming out as transgender, and the narratives that result from this practice, can be achieved." He distinguishes the two types of coming out as (a) *declaration* (an initial claiming of transgender identity) and (b) *disclosure* (sharing one's transgender history after transition). In his study, some participants used the word "disclose" for coming out, and "stealth" in place of "in the closet."[57]

As an important reality in the lives of many queer persons, coming out has been, and remains, a subject of queer theological reflection. Beyond the rigidities of immutable identities, queer theological thinking holds a view of coming out that embraces the critique of gender and sexuality as essence but holds on to the powerful religious categories of freedom, revelation, grace, honesty, and integrity as it engages the lived experiences of queer coming out. In doing so it embraces the categories of the moral, the sacred, and the political. It seeks to place in conversation theological themes from the religious tradition and the lived experience of queer lives.

The brief overview of this literature shows that, from the perspective of queer theologizing, coming out is not thought of as a singular event with repetition, but rather as an ongoing vibrant action, full of motion and open to the process of growth and development. The themes raised indicate the movement and dynamism of the process of coming out: finding a story, obeying the "natural" demand of the body for language, God revealing Godself as radical love and in the person of Jesus Christ, reconciling gender and sexual identity with one's religious tradition, living with honesty and integrity. Moreover, these actions are communal in nature, connecting identity more deeply with the family, community, culture, and tradition, which have it shaped its formation. The actions associated with the coming-out process point to the fundamental social need to

---

57. Zimman, "Other Kind of Coming Out," 53–80. The ideas cited are from pages 60–61. I am grateful to my colleague, Cameron Partridge, for directing me to this resource.

communicate with others in some sense of honesty and authenticity. This need grounds the actions of coming out in ethical practice.

Practices and Truth-telling

Since coming out remains a significant experience for many LGBTQI persons, it is important to think theologically about coming out *itself*. For persons of religious faith, the experiences of living gain meaning and purpose from their engagement with God's presence and activity in the world. The experience of coming out is no exception; however, theological thinking about coming out must not reproduce the identity essentialism and rigid gender binary of earlier conceptions. Is there a way to theologize about coming out that accepts the social construction, fluidity, and contingency of gender and sexuality?

In proposing that we think of coming out as an ethical practice, I am pointing to its potential to remove the conversation from the declaration of an essential identity that locks in a person to a category of identification. It has the capacity to create space for a more fluid and destabilized gender and sexual identity that can better respond to the complex realities of lived experience. It can leave openings for the multiple complexities of a person's social existence in community that are located in race, gender, sexuality, class, disability status, religion, and other markers of difference. As an ethical practice, it points to the moral aspects of coming out that matter to persons for whom religious meaning is significant.

This last section accomplishes three tasks. First, it articulates several key theoretical understandings of practices that ground my proposal. I have chosen to include theoretical perspectives that see practices as social, embodied, and connected to the dynamics of discourses of power. Using these same criteria, the discussion then moves to perspectives on specifically Christian understandings of practices. Finally, a discussion of the Christian practice of testimony links the action of truth-telling to religious tradition.

Practices: Theoretical Perspectives

Three philosophical perspectives on practices inform my understanding for this project: from Alasdair MacIntyre, I use the concept of "social practice," specifically in its articulation of its communal and historical attributes; from Pierre Bourdieu, I use the concept of "habitus," specifically in its articulation of the social and cultural generation of practices; from Michel Foucault, I use the concept of "disciplinary power," specifically in its implications for the way that practices are rooted in power/knowledge relations. In this brief overview of these important concepts, I hope to provide a clear intellectual grounding for the constructive use of practices as a way to think theologically about the process of coming out.

Practices Are Communal and Historical

In *After Virtue*, Alasdair MacIntyre embarks on an ambitious project to challenge Enlightenment-based, modern liberal individualism and its ethical perspectives.[58] He seeks to construct a theory of virtue that embraces the communal and historical aspects of human moral agency, in order to articulate an ultimate human goal (*telos*) rooted in social engagement. Social practice provides a fundamental starting point to his constructive effort. For the purposes of my project, his understanding of a social practice provides a basis for understanding coming out as an ethical practice.

For MacIntyre, there are three elements of a concept of virtue, which move in linear progression: practice, the narrative of a whole human life, and the engagement of that individual narrative within a communal moral tradition.[59] While I am focusing specifically on his understanding of practice, rather than a discussion of virtue specifically, it is important to note that it represents one aspect of MacIntyre's full definition of virtue.[60] He defines a practice as:

> any coherent and complex form of socially established cooperative human activity through which goods internal to that form of activity are realized in the course of trying to achieve those standards of excellence which are appropriate to, and partially definitive of, that form of activity, with the result that human powers to achieve excellence, and human conceptions of the ends and goods involved, are systematically extended.[61]

58. MacIntyre, *After Virtue*.

59. Bruce W. Ballard states that the terms "practice—narrative—tradition" encapsulates MacIntyre's concept of virtue. See Ballard, *Understanding MacIntyre*.

60. For more information see Lutz, *Reading Alasdair MacIntyre's 'After Virtue,'* 118.

61. MacIntyre, *After Virtue*, 187.

Ballard breaks down MacIntyre's theoretical definition of practice into helpful clauses: (1) a coherent, complex form of socially established cooperative activity; (2) that produces internal goods of the activity; (3) by participants striving to excel by the standards of the activity; (4) that systematically extends participants' skills and their concept of the goods and purposes of the activity.[62]

MacIntyre explains his definition further through a discussion of various aspects of practice.[63] A practice is a socially established human activity that is cooperative in nature. For example, music is an established human activity in which one learns through a social tradition. A practice is something that is complex in a way that allows it to develop over time, but that has enough coherence that it can stand alone as a specific activity. Thus, for MacIntyre, the ability to throw a football is a skill, but the ability to play football is a practice. Similarly, bricklaying is not a practice, but architecture is.

There are goods internal to a practice and one must participate in that practice to gain that internal good. MacIntyre uses the example of a child learning to play chess to make this point. At first, the child might commit to learning and winning because of an external reward, such as candy. This reason might be effective for learning chess but provides no reason for the child to not cheat in order to win. Hopefully, the child can learn through participating in the practice over time that there are better reasons for learning to play chess, for example to develop analytic skill, strategic imagination, and competitive intensity. Hopefully, through participation the child will come to an awareness of the internal good of the practice.

A practice possesses standards of excellence. A community establishes a standard of what it has come to understand over time as performing that practice in a way that indicates the highest level of achievement. This requires that one who engages the practice accepts, at least initially, the established standard in order to show competence, and accepts the guidance of those persons considered to be authorities in the practice, who embody an established understanding of excellence. One does not succeed in a practice unless a commitment to excellence is made; its moral dimension lies in that commitment to excellence.

MacIntyre makes an important distinction between the goods internal to a practice and the goods external to a practice. In the case of external

62. Ballard, *Understanding MacIntyre*, 11–12.
63. MacIntyre, *After Virtue*, 186–95.

goods, there is a competition to achieve a good, but that good is focused on an individual achievement of property or possession. With external goods excellence means more for one person and less for others. On the other hand, internal goods focus the individual achievement for the good of the community. Thus, internal goods are achieved only through social practices—engaging in practices with others over time. In addition, participation in a practice serves to develop an individual, but also to enhance the practice itself. In this way those who participate in a practice take part in advancing the development of its internal good.

Thus, from MacIntyre we establish an idea that practice involves socially established cooperative action that addresses a human need or desire by providing specific goods that are internal to the practice, and that can only be gained through participation in that practice. Committing to excellence in a practice grounds the practice in moral decision; successful achievement of excellence is built upon engagement in the shared practices of a community and tradition.

Practices Are Culturally Generated

If practices are communal and historical, then it is necessary to understand the ways in which social structures influence them. In *Outline of a Theory of Practice*, Pierre Bourdieu seeks to understand the relationship between institutions, discourses, cultural fields, worldviews, and the established actions of people in their everyday life (practices).[64] Bourdieu uses the concept of *habitus* to analyze this relationship between objective social structures and subjective actions of persons embodied in their everyday life.

He defines *habitus* as "systems of durable, transposable *dispositions* . . . principles of the generation and structuring of practices and representations which can be objectively 'regulated' and 'regular' without in any way being the product of obedience to rules . . . collectively orchestrated without being the product of the orchestrating action of a conductor."[65] He focuses on the idea of dispositions for its many connotations: a structure resulting from organizing action, a way of being, something that is related to habits, a predisposition, tendency, propensity or inclination.[66] These dispositions, embodied in everyday actions, are understood to be

64. Bourdieu, *Outline of a Theory of Practice*.
65. Bourdieu, *Outline of a Theory of Practice*, 72.
66. Bourdieu, *Outline of a Theory of Practice*, 214, note 1.

normative, but not through any specific imposition of rules; rather they are understood as a given of the culture. The *habitus*—"history turned into nature, i.e., denied as such"[67]—is embodied history that becomes understood as normative. For Bourdieu the *habitus* exist profoundly in bodies: "it is in the dialectical relationship between the body and a space structured according to the mythico-ritual oppositions that one finds the form par excellence of the structural apprenticeship which leads to the em-bodying of the structures of the world, that is, the appropriating by the world of a body thus enabled to appropriate the world."[68]

Webb, Schirato, and Donaher provide a helpful overview to Bourdieu's work.[69] They understand Bourdieu's concept of *habitus* as,

> the values and dispositions gained from our cultural history that generally stay with us across contexts (they are durable and trans-posable). These values and dispositions allow us to respond to cultural rules and contexts in a variety of ways (because they allow for improvisations), but the responses are always largely determined— regulated—by where (and who) we have been in a culture.[70]

Thus, as a result of the formative influences of our cultural history, we develop values and dispositions that we bring along to other cultural contexts in which we engage. But these values and dispositions are a product of who we have become as a result of where we come from and how we were formed by that context.

The *habitus* is not just attitudes, habits, and worldview. More specifically, it is a disposition and social relation engrained in bodies that can be seen in the way we hold our bodies, how we move, our appearance, and how we feel. It is both an embodied and dispositional reality.

The authors highlight several important aspects of the *habitus*. First, the *habitus* constructs our knowledge, worldview, beliefs, and values. We do not merely passively reproduce what we learn; rather, knowledge is formed through an active engagement of the self with social structures and social structures with the self.

Second, because of the formative influence of culture upon us we are inclined toward specific attitudes, values, and behaviors—which are capable of being brought to other cultural contexts.

67. Bourdieu, *Outline of a Theory of Practice*, 78.

68. Bourdieu, *Outline of a Theory of Practice*, 89.

69. Webb et al., *Understanding Bourdieu*, 21–44.

70. Webb et al., *Understanding Bourdieu*, 36.

Third, the *habitus* serves as the link between the socio-cultural influences and specific human practices; that is, the *habitus* develops through the embodied practices of daily life. When we confront a problem, we bring the resources of the *habitus* to bear on our action. It provides a kind of "feel for the game" that guides our action as we engage the various contexts in which we interact.

Finally, the *habitus* operates in both conscious and unconscious ways. We absorb it and it becomes part of who we are, guiding our engagement with the practices of everyday life. Constructed through social relations, the *habitus* is subjective, and reveals the conditional nature of our attitudes, values, and dispositions.

The rules and social institutions of the *habitus* come to constitute what is understood to be "human nature." They function in that way because the history, conditions, and contexts that produced them are invisible to those who embrace them: "The most crucial aspect of *habitus*, then, is that it naturalizes itself and the cultural rules, agendas, and values that make it possible."[71]

Although we have the capacity to respond with flexibility to the various rules and contexts we encounter, our responses are governed by the communities and cultures that have formed us and have made us who we are. A *habitus* does not act in a deterministic way—we have personal power and self-interest—but, deeply influential, it creates a reality in which our choices and perspectives are seen to be the standard: "in order for a particular *habitus* to function smoothly and effectively, individuals must normally think that the possibilities from which they choose are in fact, necessities, common sense, natural or inevitable."[72]

Bourdieu helps us to see that practices cannot be understood without an awareness of the *habitus* that mediates those practices with the structures of social and cultural power. The *habitus* provides a system of values, beliefs, and attitudes that assists our negotiation of daily living in specific social contexts, without necessarily fixing our action in predetermined ways.[73] However, understanding the cultural production of those disposi-

---

71. Webb et al., *Understanding Bourdieu*, 40.

72. Webb et al., *Understanding Bourdieu*, 38.

73. "The *habitus* is the universalizing mediation which causes an individual agent's practices, without either explicit reason or signifying intent, to be none the less 'sensible' and 'reasonable.'" Bourdieu, *Outline of a Theory of Practice*, 79. See also Richard Harker, Cheleen Mahar and Chris Wilkes, who state, "The central thesis to emphasize, then, is that *habitus* is a mediating construct, not a determining one." Harker et al., *An Introduction to the Work of Pierre Bourdieu*, 12.

tions creates the capacity to think critically about social practices and the unconscious prescriptions that they promote.

Practices Are Rooted in Power Relations

If practices are social, historical, and culturally generated through the *habitus*, how is personal and institutional power operating in them? Michel Foucault provides a useful analysis of how power works in the development of habits and dispositions—a fundamental component of practices—through the concept of disciplinary power: a way of "obliging subjects to repeat practices until these practices are internalized as habits and dispositions."[74]

In *The Cambridge Foucault Lexicon*, Brad Stone clarifies Foucault's distinctive understanding of practices.[75] Foucault does not understand practices as action that is the opposite of theories; rather, he understands practices metaphysically to express what is in the world, on the level of *both* theory and action. For Foucault, there is a relationship between discourse and action that the reality of practices mediates. That is, practices encompass both discourse associated with an issue and the actions that people take related to the issue: "practices determine both the way in which subjects will act and the truth claims those subjects can make."[76] In this synergy, practices form an understanding of both what a group understands to be true and how they will act, that is, practices form the worldview and the worldview forms the practices. Thus, practices have a prescriptive effect in articulating what is to be done, and a codifying effect, articulating the rules that govern understanding and action. In this way, Foucault sees that practices serve to form people into a way of life, as well as normalize it into a truth claim.

Stone discusses three types of practices in Foucault: discursive practices, practices of power, and practices of the self. In discursive practices, language, concepts, and materiality form the object about which they speak. The ways in which human beings act as subjects in the world are the practices of self. Practices of power are composed of disciplinary power and bio-political power. Disciplinary power establishes the correct methods of training people and types of activities deemed proper in a community functioning, in effect, as control over bodies. Bio-political power, or bio-power, involves governing

74. Taylor, *Routledge Guidebook*, 178.
75. Stone, "Practice."
76. Stone, "Practice," 387.

structures, such as government or religion, that normalize and enforce the established behaviors, beliefs, and actions.

Since disciplinary power influences habits and dispositions significantly, it is important to understand Foucault's understanding of power more fully. Foucault began his investigations into power first in *Discipline and Punish*.[77] In this work he examines the history of prisons and incarceration and develops connections between power and what a society considers to be truth. Disciplinary power conceptually links relationships of power to a society's production of truth. He then continues his investigation of power in *The History of Sexuality, Volume I*, where he focuses specifically on articulating a method for how to analyze society's understanding of sexual knowledge in terms of the power relations operating in that discourse.[78]

McHoul and Grace provide a useful overview of the way Foucault understands power.[79] As a first point, they see that for Foucault, rather than a universal entity, power must be understood through its instruments and techniques. They state,

> In short, Foucault suggests that power is intelligible in terms of the *techniques* through which it is exercised . . . Foucault's point is to stress that there are no *necessary* or universal forms for the exercise of power to take place: our society bears witness to the productions of quite specific practices which characterize the ways in which power relations function within it.[80]

Thus, it is important to talk about power relations, rather than a universal notion of power. The mechanisms of power relations that a society uses are what constitute disciplinary power. In addition, instruments and techniques of disciplinary power are not confined to one type of institution, rather, as techniques and instruments they can be used in any institution.[81] Surveillance is a key technique of power relations in disciplinary power. The disciplinary power creates norms that appear to be "natural" or a social given. Yet this invisibility creates a need for a compulsory visibility among

77. Foucault, *Discipline and Punish*.

78. Foucault, *History of Sexuality, Volume 1*, 92–102.

79. McHoul and Grace, *Foucault Primer*.

80. McHoul and Grace, *Foucault Primer*, 65.

81. Foucault states, "'Discipline' may be identified neither with an institution nor an apparatus; it is a type of power, a modality for its exercise, comprising a whole set of instruments, techniques, procedures, levels of application, targets; it is a 'physics' or an 'anatomy' of power, a technology." Foucault, *Discipline and Punish*, 215.

people in order for them to prove their connection to what is considered "normal."[82] The surveillance, then, serves to create a dynamic where people discipline themselves. The discipline that regulates behavior in a society or communal group serves "the normalization of individuals" and this normalization then determines the line between what is considered normal and what is considered abnormal. Thus, disciplinary power fosters obedience to the norms of a group.[83]

A second important point relates power relations and the "production" of truth in a society, or as McHoul and Grace articulate it, a connection between the techniques of power and the regimes of knowledge that are developed alongside them.[84] For Foucault, power relations and knowledge are so deeply intertwined that he refers to power specifically as power/knowledge.[85] Disciplinary power formulates knowledge according to the norms of the society or communal group. The types of instruments and procedures that are used to create a group's understanding of knowledge are central to an understanding of that knowledge.[86]

In *The History of Sexuality, Volume I*, Foucault attempts to give some definition to his understanding of power.[87] Power is "the multiplicity of force relations" that through "ceaseless struggles and confrontations" form a "chain or a system" and, as "strategies" whose designs are "embodied in the state apparatus, in the formulation of the law, in the various social hegemonies." McHoul and Grace provide a helpful articulation:

> Power is nothing more and nothing less than the multiplicity of
> force relations extant within the social body. Power's conditions

82. Foucault states, "Disciplinary power . . . is exercised through invisibility; at the same time it imposes on those whom it subjects a principle of compulsory visibility. In discipline, it is the subjects who have to be seen. Their visibility assures the hold of the power that is exercised over them." Foucault, *Discipline and Punish*, 187.

83. McHoul and Grace, *Foucault Primer*, 66–68.

84. McHoul and Grace, *Foucault Primer*, 70–71.

85. Foucault states, "We should admit rather that power produces knowledge . . . that power and knowledge directly imply one another; that there is no power relation without the correlative constitution of a field of knowledge, nor any knowledge that does not presuppose and constitute at the same time power relations . . . In short, it is not the activity of the subject of knowledge that produces a corpus of knowledge, useful or resistant to power, but power-knowledge, the processes and struggles that traverse it and of which it is made up, that determines the forms and possible domains of knowledge." Foucault, *Discipline and Punish*, 27–28.

86. McHoul and Grace, *Foucault Primer*, 70–71.

87. Foucault, *History of Sexuality, Volume 1*, 92–93.

of possibility actually consist of this moving substance of force relations: the struggles, confrontations, contradictions, inequalities, transformations and integrations of these force relations. Thus we are 'positioned' within any struggle only as a consequence of the existence of a struggle for power . . . both domination *and* resistance.[88]

Therefore, there is not one group with power and one without. Power is relational and comes from all segments of a society. Different tactics are employed depending upon a group or person's position in a power struggle. The various tactics of the instruments of power get coordinated into coherent power strategies, which are used by specific groups.

Chloë Taylor articulates the main features of Foucault's understanding of power.[89] First, power is omnipresent; it is everywhere. Everyone exercises the power of enforcing social norms (disciplinary power), and they exercise it over each other.

Second, power is war—that is, it is more useful to think of power in terms of the dynamics of warfare, than in terms of sovereignty, dominion or law. Similar to military planning, power involves strategies and tactics.

Third, power is relational. Power is not something that we have, share or lose; rather, people exist in shifting networks of power. These relationships are non-egalitarian in that some people are in more privileged positions of power within the shifting relations that exist within structures of inequalities in a society. Taylor states, "power relations are always moving and complex, and no one is completely powerless within them; in situations of dominance in which one individual is completely subordinated to another, Foucault argues that we are talking about violence rather than power."[90]

Fourth, power is immanent. It exists in all relationships, including government and law, but also, pedagogical, sexual, and romantic relationships.

Fifth, power comes from below the official structures of power. We typically understand that power comes from a top-down direction. For Foucault, power come from daily relationships that consciously and unconsciously enforce normalizing behavior which then moves through society.

Sixth, power relations are intentional and non-subjective. Foucault means that even though there are moments by that people self-consciously

88. McHoul and Grace, *Foucault Primer*, 84.

89. Taylor, *Routledge Guidebook*, 55–71.

90. Taylor, *Routledge Guidebook*, 59.

use calculations and strategies, there is not an overarching plan that controls action. There are always ways in which people cannot foresee the effects of actions that are taken in specific circumstances.

Seventh, power produces resistance. In fact, resistance is another aspect of power; there exists both the power of domination and the power of resistance. Taylor states,

> Foucault describes resistance as an outcome of power that happens to people rather than as something that people engage in. Resistance is something inevitable or automatic: it is not that we may or may not *choose* to resist power but, rather, that resistance will always arise *wherever* there is power, and it will do so whether we *want* to resist or not.[91]

Foucault remained unclear about the topic of resistance and did not articulate exactly what he understood that resistance to look like. However, with this statement Foucault creates in his theorizing a space for the development of subjectivity, agency, and responsibility in the ways in which people are engaged in power relations.

Practices and Coming Out

In this brief overview of several philosophical perspectives on practices, I have tried to show that practices are part of a community and a tradition, but that we must think critically about the normalizing functions of those practices as they function in our lives. We cannot receive them uncritically without understanding that normative practices serve to create community and group coherence that can function in exclusionary ways that can restrict human freedom to act in ways that feel authentic to a person. To understand coming out as a practice, we must attend to not only its communal and historical elements, but also to the power dynamics that exist in the creation of habits and dispositions, and that consciously or unconsciously restrict the articulation of truth-telling. With this foundation, we move to a discussion of specifically Christian-based practices.

91. Taylor, *Routledge Guidebook*, 67–68.

Christian Faith Practices

Within Christian traditions, practices provide a way to speak theologically about coming out that resonates with its dynamic, fluid energy, embodied reality, and situatedness in discourses of power. Craig Dykstra and Dorothy C. Bass, deeply influenced by MacIntyre's understanding of social practices, provide a helpful definition: "Christian practices are things Christian people do together over time in response to and in light of God's active presence for the life of the world in Christ Jesus."[92] Specifically, they focus on twelve practices that are consistent with this definition: honoring the body, hospitality, household economics, saying yes and saying no, keeping Sabbath, testimony, discernment, shaping communities, forgiveness, healing, dying well, singing our lives. These practices are ordinary activities that are focused in Christian purpose, responding to God's presence in the community and in the world. When "woven together," the practices "suggest the patterns of a Christian way of life" that respond to contemporary realities.[93]

Christian practices have several important characteristics.[94] First, "Practices address fundamental human needs and conditions through concrete human acts." Practices have a deeply practical purpose and seek to address embodied human needs at a basic level. In doing actions that help humanity and the rest of creation flourish, people cooperate with God in responding to needs.

Second, "Practices are done together and over time." These practices have been done in communities over centuries, sometimes well and sometimes poorly, but with critical conversation about how to live these practices out in ways that are more faithful to their intention. Importantly, while each practice is connected to the Christian tradition, they are not fixed and static. Rather, they are contextual, adaptive, and evolving in the light of specific communities, cultures, and traditions.

Third, "Practices possess standards of excellence." The actions of engaging in practices must be critically assessed to ensure that they are faithful to their intention and to the theological tradition that they are representing. For Dykstra and Bass, "This process is important. Because practices are so

---

92. Dykstra and Bass, "Times of Yearning, Practices of Faith," 5.
93. Dykstra and Bass, "Times of Yearning, Practices of Faith," 5.
94. Dykstra and Bass, "Times of Yearning, Practices of Faith," 6–8.

spacious and flexible, we need to be prepared to think about what it means to do them well rather than badly."[95]

Finally, the ordinary activities of practices reveal the way in which "our daily lives are all tangled up with the things God is doing in the world." These ordinary activities of life are transformed in their connection to God's practices for renewing human communities and all creation.

For Dykstra and Bass, practices that are Christian are distinctive in their normative and theological claims: "The distinctive understanding of *Christian practices* . . . focuses on practices as the constitutive elements in a way of life that becomes incarnate when human beings live in the light of and in response to God's gift of life abundant."[96] Thus, there is a presumption that embodied practices address fundamental human needs in a way that is connected to God's creating and sustaining the world through the reconciling action of Jesus. Christian people participate in and come to understand in more depth God's plan and purpose for creation through engagement in Christian practices.

Dykstra and Bass's definition of Christian practices does not sufficiently challenge the ways in which practices, necessarily open and flexible in articulation and implementation, are constructions of dominant discourses in a religious tradition, culture, or society. Kathryn Tanner, building upon Dykstra and Bass in their understanding of Christian practices, uses an approach from social science that examines the ways in which Christian practices are open-ended and culturally determined, and therefore, necessarily require the rigorous critical assessment that theological reflection provides: "To see the importance of theology for everyday Christian life, one must understand how theological inquiry is forced by the vagaries of Christian practices themselves and is, consequently, a necessary part of their ordinary functioning."[97] Theologians, in their attempts to make sense of the actions and beliefs of Christian commitments, often seek to establish common values or to construct norms for communities. In the process, they "tend to fix and strictly delimit Christian practices—for example, by offering rules or codes by which they abide."[98] As theologians develop systems of ideas, they also connect those ideas to actions and beliefs in the tradition. This

95. Dykstra and Bass, "Times of Yearning, Practices of Faith," 8.

96. Dykstra and Bass, "Theological Understanding of Christian Practices."

97. Tanner, "Theological Reflection and Christian Practices," 228.

98. Tanner, "Theological Reflection and Christian Practices," 229.

creates an impression that Christianity and the practices that express it are self-evident and given. She explains,

> Theologians construct systems of ideas and draw systemic connections between Christian action and beliefs. Thus, beliefs about God and the world seamlessly suggest the propriety of certain courses of Christian action, and these actions supply the social circumstances that make those beliefs seem natural.[99]

In the theoretical abstraction of reflection, Christian action can become grounded in an isolated logic that validates each idea. Christian action comes from a Christian belief—at least that is the simplified way it can look without the benefit of the critical assessment of theological reflection.

Since Christian practices are open-ended and always in the process of adapting themselves in response to specific circumstances, many beliefs, actions, and values do not cohere well. She understands this fact as part of the nature of practices themselves:

> Christian practices tend to be like this because practices generally are. In general, practices, especially when they involve ongoing forms of coordinated social action on a large scale, simply do not require a great deal of reflective depth for their common functioning . . . Rather than having a rigidly fixed structure, practices in general are fluid and processional in nature, working through improvisation and ad hoc response to changing circumstances.[100]

For example, a diverse church community might be able to function smoothly in the practice of Holy Communion, without all members agreeing to the meaning and rationale of their actions. Practices can be inconsistent, and beliefs and practices can be loosely related to each other.

At the same time, the ambiguous and inconsistent aspects of Christian practices are exactly what makes them able to support a Christian way of life in a complex and unpredictable world. In order for practices to work effectively, they must be subject to a critical reflection process that helps them to become more consistent and coherent as expressions of the action of God in the world: "The ambiguities, inconsistencies, and open-endedness of Christian practice are . . . the very things that establish an essential place for theological reflection in everyday Christian lives . . . because Christian practices are like this, they will not work without critical theological

99. Tanner, "Theological Reflection and Christian Practices," 229.
100. Tanner, "Theological Reflection and Christian Practices," 230.

engagement."[101] Practices need deliberate reflective efforts to make judgments about effective action. Thus, theological reflection is a necessary process in the functioning of practices in everyday life.

Taken together, these two works point to an understanding of Christian practices that is both grounded in the religious tradition of Christianity over history, and judiciously aware of the ways in which those religious discourses need to be critically assessed and implemented for effective judgment to thrive.

The Practice of Testimony

Returning to the question of coming out and religious practices, I propose that the Christian practice of testimony connects coming out as truth-telling to the Christian tradition and provides a grounding for coming out as ethical practice. Coming out is truth-telling from the Christian practice of testimony.

The word testimony raises legal images of a courtroom where there is a declaration of a witness who is under oath to tell the truth about whatever is in question, providing evidence in support of facts. A testimony can also be a public declaration of a religious experience or belief. In each context, declarations of truth are the lifeblood of the interaction. Truth-telling—and the expectation of hearing truthful words—links these two worlds.

Thomas G. Long provides a helpful understanding of testimony, and its related word witness, from a Christian perspective. He views testimony as the action of "putting the Christian faith into words out in the everyday arenas of life."[102] He believes that to see testimony as only related to Christian conversion processes limits its power. Rather, testimony involves being able to speak truthfully about the reality of the world and God's presence in creating and sustaining it. Testifying seeks first to understand and acknowledge God's work in the world, and then join with God in that activity. God is speaking to the world, and thus, with testimony religious persons are speaking in collaboration with God's speaking: "If God is talking out there in the world, then we are to be talking too. We are to talk as God talks. That is the essence of testimony."[103]

---

101. Tanner, "Theological Reflection and Christian Practices," 232.

102. Long, *Talking Ourselves into Being Christian*, 27.

103. Long, *Talking Ourselves into Being Christian*, 74.

What are the characteristics of testimony? First, testimony is a social action in which a public declaration is made. For Thomas Hoyt Jr., testimony is a communally based practice that requires the presence of witnesses to speak truthfully and others who can receive it and evaluate its veracity. Thus, testimony is a "deeply shared practice—one that is possible only in a community that recognizes that falsehood is strong, but yearns nonetheless to know what is true and good."[104]

Another characteristic of testimony relates to how its truth-telling necessarily exists as an action within relational boundaries in human community, and thus, requires wisdom in its usage. Both strategically and morally, testimony is diminished when its usage creates misunderstanding or foments divisiveness. Testimony can be either a statement or a document, but in either case it is more readily understood by its effect than its declaration. As Long states,

> So when is telling the whole truth a good thing, and when is it not? Over the generations, Christians have learned that the kind of truth we are most interested in, the kind of truth we are most called to tell, is measured not only by what it is but also by what it does. In Christian terms, truth is more like a verb than a noun. It causes things to happen. Christians, then, are not just concerned to get the facts straight and to put the bald truth on the table. They are alert to timing, effects, and relationships.[105]

It is the verb-like action of testimony that makes it a truth that is alive and engaged in human interaction as a moral action. Relationally, testimony must speak truth, but it must be used in a way that respects how that truth is received in communities.[106]

Integrity—in the sense of honesty, consistency, and accuracy in representation of oneself through words and actions—fundamentally characterizes testimony. Mary E. Hunt has long advocated for an ethical stance that values the quality of the sexual relationships that people engage in—their integrity—rather than focusing on the specific gender pairings. In *Fierce Tenderness: A Feminist Theology of Friendship*, she seeks to construct theo-ethical

---

104. Hoyt, "Testimony," 90.

105. Long, *Talking Ourselves into Being Christian*, 99.

106. It is important to note that testimony, while often related to the action of speaking words, can also occur through silence and through bodily action. The truth-telling of coming out is not restricted to the testimony of words alone.

norms that are based on the model of friendship, rather than on coupling.[107] In another work, she argues for "sexual integrity" as a "constructive alternative" to a focus on essentialist identity categories: "By using 'sexual integrity' I mean to sidestep the still unanswerable questions of why people love as they do, and move on to what we do know, namely, that most people do the best they can to love well . . . I observe that it is integrity, not preference, orientation or identity, with which we ought to be concerned."[108]

An important aspect of integrity concerns critical awareness of the ways in which the language of testimony exists with the constructs of social and cultural ways of knowing and conveying experiences. In other words, the integrity of testimony requires an understanding that its articulation is not from an internal essence, but rather, is mediated through cultural expressions of meaning-making. Mark D. Jordan views testimony (along with counterargument, fragmentary history and provocative analogy) as one "shape for truth-telling."[109] He reminds his readers that the integrity of testimony must be understood as existing within the boundaries of defined genres, but that, nevertheless, still hold power. He states,

> There are complications in testimony. When we tell coming out stories, we are not giving raw experience, however raw the telling feels. We fit our stories into increasingly well defined genres, into cultural patterns for storytelling. If we want to rely on individual testimonies in truth telling, we should of course admit they are edited by understandable motives and by inherited narrative patterns. So is every act of human speech. We need to be sophisticated when we cite individual testimony, but that doesn't mean that we give it up altogether.[110]

Specifically referring to the context of the Roman Catholic Church, Jordan believes that the testimony of truth-telling about queer lives is both necessary for personal integrity and an important basis of information about the existence and practices of queer lives in the church.

---

107. Hunt states, "A friendship norm implies new patterns of relating that reflect values of love and justice lived out not two by heterosexual two, but in many combinations of genders and in three, fours, and dozens as well. This is what it means to call for a new relational ethic based on friendships, lots of them. It assumes that we will be just as rigorous in our evaluation of friendship as others have been dogmatic in their condemnation of anything that did not approximate their coupling." Hunt, *Fierce Tenderness*, 14.

108. Hunt, "Sexual Integrity," 1–3.

109. Jordan, *Telling Truths in Church*, 15.

110. Jordan, *Telling Truths in Church*, 15.

Thus, the practice of testimony, in its diverse forms of expression, con-nects truth-telling to coming out. In fact, the very idea of testimony creates an expectation of hearing and witnessing truthfulness. From the perspective of Christian faith, testimony creates an obligation to speak truthfully about the world and about God's engagement with and in the world. Testimony is a social action, but cannot be used as a weapon of discord, and be considered a moral action. Rather, it must be used to build up community in ways that serve to create a better world. Finally, integrity is a fundamental characteris-tic of testimony; however, it is important to assess critically how integrity is defined and experienced through social and cultural influences.

Concluding Thoughts

Admittedly, this chapter has made its way through a diverse list of intel-lectual resources and influences. This diversity seems necessary when considering the messy reality of queer lived experience. It presents several ideas that together create a rationale for an understanding of coming out as an ethical practice.

First, coming out cannot be realistically understood to be the expres-sion of a hidden, inner essence of an individual self. At the same time, coming out is undeniably present in queer lived experience and can be un-derstood as an important aspect of queer religious and spiritual experience. Second, thinking of coming out as a practice creates a bridge between the important challenges to an essentialist idea of self, and the lived reality of many queer religious experiences that are related to the experience of com-ing out. Third, understanding coming out as a practice of truth-telling, of testimony, makes space for both the real need to be known in some authen-tic way in community (with its existence of norms and disciplinary power that can restrict human freedom) and the real need to live out the reality of our becoming-selfhood-in-relation, with a freedom that understands the fluidity, performativity, and constructed nature of who we are and how we engage religious and spiritual experiences.

Returning to the themes that began this chapter, we can say that coming out as the practice of truth-telling challenges the existence of the "mythical norm" that Audre Lorde resisted. Challenging the "mythical norm" embraces coming out as an act of disruptive coherence. What does that resistance look like? What are the component parts of the concept of disruptive coherence? This is the constructive task toward which we now turn.

4

Developing Disruptive Coherence

*I*n previous chapters I sought to make the case that coming out can be understood as the erotic ethical practice of truth-telling—from a Christian perspective it is related to the practice of testimony. Coming out as a practice of truth-telling avoids the trap of becoming a repetitive revelation of a hidden reified identity. Practices, which develop and change over time and are specific within a variety of social differences, make space for the vibrant motion of an ongoing becoming-selfhood-in-relation that takes into account the social context of lived experience. They also have standards and agreed-upon norms that can be reinterpreted as the practices grow and develop. Grounded in specific religious communities and traditions, practices are alive with the capacity to reflect and express the intersectional realities of discourses related to race, gender, class, disability status, and other markers of otherness. To be sure practices can exclude and reify normativities that, unless they are critically examined, can cause harm. Coming out understood as the erotic ethical practice of truth-telling aims to "keep it real" so that the concrete circumstances of our lives become included in how we negotiate the fluidity of being out and being in the closet, disclosure and hiddenness, revelation and covering. It engages the intersectional discourses of social power that are part of lived experience. It helps queer persons to live in a world with personal authenticity that resists the systems that seek to discipline and punish transgression from the norm.

In the next chapters, I seek to sketch out the dynamic components of coming out as truth-telling. Earlier I have referred to this energy as disruptive coherence; I now seek to explain it more fully. The current chapter aims to develop the building blocks of disruptive coherence, with specific attention to the formation of conscience and the practice of discernment. The next chapter aims to define disruptive coherence more specifically, as well as to consider some important aspects of it in queer lived experience.

Finally, I want to state clearly some of the assumptions and beliefs that are at the heart of this constructive turn. I believe that God is the source of life, and that as created beings, humans are made in ways that connect us deeply to the Divine and to divine purposes. As both physical bodies and divinely infused spirit, humans exist in a reality that is both embodied and spiritually animated. The psalmist states it poetically: "For it was you who formed my inward parts; you knit me together in my mother's womb. I praise you for I am fearfully and wonderfully made."[1]

In the dynamic engagement of freedom, resistance, spiritual centeredness in God, bodily awareness, and relationships of culture and community, human beings come to understand and develop a personal authenticity about the many ways that love can be expressed truthfully in one's life. For queer persons within the confines of heteronormative discourses of power, learning to listen to the wisdom of the body and its desires, the wisdom of a God-centered spirit, and the wisdom of culture and community has the capacity to focus and direct an understanding of what constitutes genuine expressions of love in our lives. In short, I assume that the diverse expressions of queer loving—expressions that are genuine and authentically lived[2]—can become understood in queer lives from our discernment of our bodily, spiritual, and communal wisdom.

This wisdom infuses our actions as a vital aspect of our becoming-selfhood-in-relation. We are created by God *and* we are responsible to commit to the ongoing process of developing our queer subjectivity. This reality helps us to articulate a middle ground between perspectives that might be viewed as opposite to each other.

---

1. Ps 139:13–14a, NRSV.

2. I am thinking here of Judith Butler's challenge to what she considers a "bad reading" of her notion of performativity: "The bad reading goes something like this: I can get up in the morning, look in my closet, and decide which gender I want to be today. I can take out a piece of clothing and change my gender, stylize it, and then that evening I can change it again and be something radically other, so that what you get is something like the commodification of gender, and the understanding of taking on gender as a kind of consumerism." Kotz, "Body You Want," 83. See also, Butler, *Bodies that Matter*, ix: "For if I were to argue that genders are performative, that could mean that I thought that one woke in the morning, perused the closet or some other open space for the gender of choice, donned that gender for the day, and then restored the garment to its place at night. Such a willful and instrumental subject, one who decides *on* its gender, is clearly not its gender from the start and fails to realize that its existence is already decided *by* gender."

For example, from the perspective of trans theology, Justin Tanis challenges the binary between "created and creating."[3] For him, the idea that trans persons exist in the tension between "being created and being a co-creator" opens up the possibility of new theological ways of thinking beyond binaries: "As trans people we should take seriously the task of creating for ourselves the lives to which we feel called and compelled . . . When we see this process as sacred, we can claim our places as artists cooperating with God in creating the developing changing person that we are becoming."[4]

In clarifying my assumptions, I want to open up the middle spaces between belief in a God-created queer "self" and awareness of the ways in which we construct and perform our queer subjectivities and becoming-selfhood in the reality of living.

Truth-telling and the Erotic

Why is coming out as truth-telling an *erotic* ethical practice? As stated previously, truth-telling is itself an ethical practice connected to the practice of testimony, so what does it mean to say that it is an *erotic* ethical practice? These are useful questions to consider because they point to a central spiritual grounding of empowered queer living: experiences of the erotic are sacred features of human embodiment that lead one toward the divine, toward God.

Donald Boisvert understands the energy of queer spirituality to be "an affirmation of sexuality":

> If most major religious traditions emphasize procreation as the prime end of sexual intercourse, a queer spirituality looks rather to desire as its one overarching and compelling dynamic. There are no inhibitions or hidden agendas about this. If it were not for this affirmation of the erotic as both necessary and central to the spiritual life and to any genuine experience of the sacred, then queer spirituality would really have no reason to exist. . . . Bodies like ours, our responses to them, and our desire for them: these are the real and vital components of a queer spirituality. . . . It understands the erotic as a privileged path to the divine.[5]

3. Tanis, *Trans-Gendered*, 182–83.
4. Tanis, *Trans-Gendered*, 182.
5. Boisvert, "Homosexuality and Spirituality," 36–37.

Queer spiritual energy seeks to bring together sensuality and the sacred in ways that affirm divine engagement in queer bodies and queer lives. Queer bodies embrace erotic energy as a way to become more deeply connected to the Holy.[6] Therefore, *erotic* ethical practices affirm and support an understanding of the positive presence and sacred importance of the erotic in queer bodies and queer living.

Earlier theological positions, specifically from identified lesbian feminist perspectives—which Elizabeth Stuart refers to as "erotic theology"[7]—sought to challenge negative notions of the erotic, understanding it as power for the creation of right relationships in our societies and in our relations. In particular, Carter Heyward's work significantly impacted theological discussions involving the redefinition of the relationship of sexuality and the sacred.

Heyward was deeply influenced by Audre Lorde's classic essay, "The Uses of the Erotic: The Erotic as Power" in developing her own theological positions. For Lorde, the erotic is power, "an assertion of the lifeforce of women; of that creative energy empowered, the knowledge and use of which we are now reclaiming in our language, our history, our dancing, our loving, our work, our lives."[8] Building upon Lorde's idea, Heyward describes the erotic as "power in right relation"[9] with "mutuality" as "the experience of being in right relation."[10] Justice is the expression of that mutuality in right relation. For Heyward, "Justice is the shape of mutuality in our life together, in our societies and relationships . . . Justice is the actual shape of love in the world."[11] Furthermore, she understands that relational power as the Sacred: "God is our relational power. God is born in this relational power. God is becoming our power insofar as we are giving birth to this sacred Spirit in the quality of our lives in relation, the authenticity of our mutuality, the strength of our relational matrix."[12] Coming out is important

6. I want to clarify here that I am not making the claim that only queer bodies embrace erotic energy as a way to connect sensuality and the sacred. As Margaret Kamitsuka makes clear, feminist, womanist, and queer theologians have been rethinking the role of the erotic and its connection to the sacred in theology and ethics. See note 40 in this chapter.

7. Stuart, *Gay and Lesbian Theologies*, 51–63.

8. Lorde, *Sister Outsider*, 55.

9. Heyward, *Touching Our Strength*, 3.

10. Heyward, *Touching Our Strength*, 191.

11. Heyward, *Touching Our Strength*, 190–91.

12. Heyward, *Touching Our Strength*, 24.

in her thinking precisely because it embodies each person's participation in the creation of this relational power, which is the erotic, which is God:[13] "There is great power in naming ourselves. For you to come out will contribute to the well-being of us all insofar as you are participating in shaping the Sacred among us."[14] It is this truth-telling agency that communally creates the relational power of God among all.

The work of Marcella Althaus-Reid—whose theology engaged Queer Theory, Liberation Theology, post-Marxist and Postcolonial theories—developed theological considerations of the erotic to explicitly embrace bodies, sensualities, sex, and erotic desires as the substance of theologizing in a liberationist mode. She challenged liberation theology's inattention to the compulsory gender and sexual codes of "decency" that disempower women. These codes, "the sexual organization of the public and private spaces of society," serve to construct and enforce "a moral order which is based on a heterosexual order of reality, which organizes not only categories of approved social and divine interactions but of economic ones too."[15] She proposes "Indecent Theology" as theologizing that deconstructs the discourses of decency that have subjugated women:

> Indecent Theology is a theology which problematizes and undresses the mythical layers of multiple oppression in Latin America, a theology which, finding its point of departure at the crossroads of Liberation Theology and Queer Thinking, will reflect on theological and economic oppression with passion and impudence. An Indecent Theology will question the traditional Latin American field of decency and order as it permeates and supports the multiple (ecclesiological, theological, political and amatory) structures of life in my country, Argentina, and in my continent.[16]

For Althaus-Reid, doing theology from the perspective of the embodied sexual experiences of poor women challenges liberation theology to unmask the heterosexual discourses of power that are used to regulate and control women. It requires of the theologian a sexual honesty that does not forget the concrete experiences of women's lives when doing theology—"to

13. Stuart makes an important critique about what she views as problematic ways in which Heyward connects the erotic and God. Such a discussion is beyond the scope of the present work, but is, nonetheless, an important critical perspective in considering Heyward's thought. See Stuart, *Gay and Lesbian Theologies*, 54–56.

14. Heyward, *Touching Our Strength*, 24.

15. Althaus-Reid, *Indecent Theology*, 1–2.

16. Althaus-Reid, *Indecent Theology*, 2.

be able to reflect with theological honesty on issues of women, economic struggle, images of God and the flow of sexual desires."[17] The honesty she demands is a "kind of coming out process," a truth-telling that "disrobes the underwear of heterosexual theology" to reveal its biases and subjugating power.[18] To find God outside of heterosexual theology requires "theological queering" that facilitates "the coming out of the closet of God," so that we can understand the God who is not defined by heterosexual experiences, producing a theology that disempowers all who do not fit within its prescribed constructs.[19]

The work of Heyward and Althaus-Reid, although different in their theological approaches and understanding of the self as a stable identity, point to an understanding of bodies and their erotic desires as a way to interrupt the exclusivity of heterosexually normative theological constructs. Such an idea is fundamental to the development of disruptive coherence because it embraces the disruptions of truth-telling as an ethical practice that is necessary for a queer connection to God.

The truth-telling of queer bodies and queer desires connects the erotic to the idea of coming out as disruptive coherence. Queer desire disrupts the exclusive norms of heterosexual love and becomes a moral action of becoming queer selfhood—expressing the transgressive truth-telling of queer loving. It is in the transgressive body-knowledge of queer desire that testimony and the erotic are joined in an action of queer moral agency. Queer body-knowledge, combined with a communally grounded God-centeredness, helps to create and sustain the convictions that form coming out as erotic ethical practice. It is an ethical practice that honors and incorporates the wisdom of body-knowledge, the wisdom of God's animating spirit in one's life and the wisdom of communities.

The truth-telling of coming out as disruptive coherence makes transparent queer passion in the world and has the capacity to become what Ronald E. Long refers to as "spiritual testimony," whereby bodies take a stand, both literally and metaphorically, to bring into motion queer agency and subjectivity.[20]

---

17. Althaus-Reid, *Indecent Theology*, 5.
18. Althaus-Reid, *Indecent Theology*, 19.
19. Althaus-Reid, *Queer God*, 2.
20. Long, "One Gay Man's Trinitarian Faith," 216–18.

Towards Erotic Ethical Practices of Truth-telling

John J. McNeill, arguably one of the great "saints" of early gay and lesbian theology,[21] challenged gay and lesbian persons (the language and thinking used in his time) to develop spiritual maturity as a way to resist what he saw as "the fallibility of religious authority" that could ethically undermine actions of personal conscience. He meant this specifically in the context of his understanding of gay and lesbian identity and the religious teachings that viewed it as immoral. He states,

> we are dependent on the fallibility of religious authorities in order to develop an adult freedom of conscience. When we gays and lesbians discover that we cannot follow the fallible teachings of our religious authorities without destroying ourselves, then we are forced to search out what God is saying to us through our experience and take personal responsibility for the choices we make.[22]

Furthermore, McNeill suggests that spiritual maturity is based on a primary principle: "resist and refuse to perform any religious observance that is based exclusively on fear of God!"[23]

His challenge to push back against those fear-based practices that can destroy spiritual and psychological health are significant to an understanding of the erotic ethical practices that develop disruptive coherence. Such resistance forces queer becoming-selfhood-in-relation to encounter and make sense of the wisdom of diverse gender and sexual experiences, varying bodies, and unconventional connections to God.

Although theological thinking has critiqued the limitations apparent in McNeill's modernist sense of the autonomous true self that needs to be claimed as a prerequisite for spiritual and psychological maturity,[24] I would argue that the intent of his understanding rings true even today. Queer persons can be powerfully assisted in developing their becoming-selfhood-in-relation through the spiritual maturity of (a) understanding the spiritual movement of God in their lived experience that empowers responsible freedom and (b) engaging that power and channeling it in order to transgress normativities that disconnect them from responsible freedom.

---

21. See Part 2 for Festschrift articles honoring McNeill's life and work in McNeill, *Sex As God Intended.*

22. McNeill, *Freedom, Glorious Freedom,* 11.

23. McNeill, *Taking a Chance on God,* 8.

24. See for example, Stuart, *Gay and Lesbian Theologies,* 19–20.

Developing deeply-held ethical convictions, formed from individual and communal engagement with God and that are not based in fear, are fundamental to the work of developing disruptive coherence. Developing a spiritual maturity helps to clarify those ethical convictions and creates a relationship with God that gives perspective to view with critical awareness the ways in which disciplinary power works to compel adherence to compulsory norms. Developing ethical convictions can empower acts of resistance to transgress oppressive normativities.

Developing spiritual maturity is, therefore, necessary for queer ethical agency in the following way: *The regulating discourses that seek to destroy deeply held ethical convictions about queer subjectivity and agency, especially as based in a fear of God, are challenged and resisted through the power of listening deeply to and acting upon individual and communal spiritual movements and experiences of God that lead to responsible freedom.* The honesty and strength of these ethical convictions can empower coming out as the practice of truth-telling. Acknowledging the power of such convictions, formed in the interdependency and accountability of living in cultural and communal relationships, thus becomes a significant starting point to understanding the erotic ethical practices of disruptive coherence.

It is important to remember, however (as stated in the last chapter), that ethical convictions are shaped from social ethical practices that are also culturally formed and function as disciplinary power that controls and regulates. Therefore, ethical practices, the convictions they form, and the theological and biblical interpretations that support them must be critically examined to discern whether they lead to responsible freedom and positive acceptance of queer humanity. The distinction between ethical practices that empower queer freedom and those that suffocate it—understood in its multiplicities of experiences and nuances of meanings—can be seen in the degree to which they empower in LGBTQI persons responsible freedom, positive acceptance of body and erotic desire, and deeper connection to the holy.

My understanding of the erotic ethical practices that are central in the process of coming out as truth-telling emerges experientially from an earlier work in which I reflect on my own experience of coming out through the Spiritual Exercises of Saint Ignatius, a spiritual practice of the Roman Catholic tradition. In this work I concluded with a statement that has energized my focus on the ethical practices of Christian traditions:

In its capacity to reveal the ways in which queer Christians live
and thrive with the aid of religious practices, practical theology
from a queer perspective makes an important contribution to the
development of queer theology. It allows us to see what might be
the queerest statement of all: the tradition itself holds the power of
transgression and transformation within its own practices.[25]

My sense of the radical and transgressive possibilities of the practices of
Christian traditions are at the heart of developing disruptive coherence. It
leads me to engage ethical practices that help to build transgressive convictions of becoming-selfhood-in-relation, formed through embracing the
wisdom of body-knowledge, the wisdom of God's animating spirit in one's
life and the wisdom of communities.

Disruptive Coherence as Moral Formation

As an idea, disruptive coherence has less to do with abstract theory and
more to do with developing convictions that empower truth-telling. I suggest that it is a process of moral formation of conscience, although not one
based on transmitting systematized ethical precepts. Rather, the moral
formation occurs through the action of learning how to be ethical. Ethical
practices are among the ways that we learn to act in moral ways. These ways
of learning might include, for example, the sacred scriptures of a tradition,
examples of significant persons in one's life, and of course, the formalized
moral precepts of a religious or spiritual community.

Yet, there is a contestation inherent in ethical practices. They both
shape understandings of morality according to dominant normativities
and, also, require ongoing critique to ensure that the shaping be an ethic
of justice that is inclusive of multiple human experiences. Values shape individuals and communities; there is no avoiding it. Critique and resistance
can challenge values that are exclusive of multiple human experiences and
create greater inclusivity. The moral formation of disruptive coherence
must keep this tension in place, and cannot revert, uncritically, to a normalizing discourse that does not engage multiplicity.

Mark D. Jordan's understanding of moral formation in Thomas Aquinas influences my own thinking about this tension. In *Teaching Bodies: Moral Formation in the* Summa *of Thomas Aquinas*, Jordan reads through the
Summa in order to discover what he understands to be "misreading" of the

25. Talvacchia, "Disrupting the Theory-Practice Binary," 194.

text: "My concern is not so much with mistakes in construing terms, syntax, images or arguments. The mistakes that matter most are distorted relations to Thomas's whole effort of teaching. They often result from approaching the text with the wrong assumptions about how and what it teaches."[26] One cause of the misreading he understands to be a failure of contemporary readers to negotiate the ways in which the text is "official, antiquated, and demanding."[27] That is, readers bring to it (a) preconceived ideas about its official interpretation, (b) a failure to take into account the ways in which it contains a significant amount of outdated terms, science, and reasoning, and (c) a failure to understand the moral demands it makes on its readers. For Jordan, to read Thomas responsibly one must negotiate between "its pedagogical hopes and our diverse dispositions," which will lead to different results because of the multiple experiences of humans.[28]

He devises an ingenious method for his exegesis. He views the *Summa* as a "progressive pedagogy" rather than as a listing of systematic deductions: "It is a curriculum that encourages and represents learning across time—the time of present reasoning about authorities from various past times."[29] He sees the structure of the *Summa* as a pedagogy to form teachers who will possess maturity in their reasoning about and articulation of morality. How can a contemporary reader enter into a moral curriculum that was designed in a specific historical time, for a particular purpose, that has been generalized over time by religious communities? He chooses to read the text in reverse order:

> If you read the *Summa* beginning with its last part, you begin with the incarnation, the life of Christ, and the Christian sacraments as continuations of that life. For Thomas, moral formation ultimately depends on these scenes of embodied instruction—not on assent to abstract 'principles' from which one attempts to make binding deductions. We learn the best way to teach human beings by watching how God taught us. God did not send down a numbered list of moral axioms or a crisply formulated universal imperative. God took flesh. Embodied souls learn through bodies and from bodies. They learn from particular scenes enacted in time.[30]

26. Jordan, *Teaching Bodies*, vii–viii.

27. Jordan, *Teaching Bodies*, vii.

28. Jordan, *Teaching Bodies*, ix.

29. Jordan, *Teaching Bodies*, 11.

30. Jordan, *Teaching Bodies*, 15.

This strategy helps him to see the *Summa* as a text of embodied pedagogy that is taught with practical intent, by bodies and to bodies, through engaging the embodied event of an incarnational God engaged in human experience.

What is the significance of Thomas's pedagogy for moral formation? For Jordan, if humans learn best through an embodied moral instruction, then ethics must attempt to engage human lives in its work: "It is called to speak about embodiment, not despite it."[31]

Jordan's ideas are an important grounding for understanding the way in which ethical practices develop disruptive coherence as a moral formation of conscience. Ethical practices must engage the multiple experiences of bodies in communities in order to subvert the normalizing tendencies of moral formation. In disruptive coherence the embodied learning of ethical practices shapes moral agency to engage in embodied truth-telling—embodied testimony. *Coming out as the erotic ethical practice of truth-telling is an embodied testimony fueled with the morally formative energy of disruptive coherence.*

Values and Ethical Practices of Embodied Testimony

This next section, part of a larger project on which I am working, sketches out some of the values and ethical practices that develop the moral formation of disruptive coherence. As a work in progress, I do not propose them as system of ideas comprising an argument. I propose them, rather, as an act of moral imagination with the energy of disruptive coherence. In queering some established ideas related to moral formation, I want to imagine possible strategies that might interrupt their typical understandings. I want to reflect upon various ways that we might live into ethical convictions that can support the action of coming out as embodied testimony. I see these values and practices as a process that invites critical reflective engagement on how one might live the complexity of becoming-selfhood-in-relation within the pushes and pulls of social discourses of power.

What values might support a developing queer moral agency? Two embodied actions are at the heart of disruptive coherence and ground its convictions in specific values: *prioritizing justice-love* and *honoring communal relationships.*

31. Jordan, *Teaching Bodies*, 64.

As a relational action, coming out as the ethical practice of truth-telling seeks to encompass in its movements the characteristics of just relations: right relationships of power, mutuality, and fairness that take into account the material and social realities that encompass people's lives. The truth-telling of coming out cannot be achieved in the context of unjust relationships. It is achieved in the context of what Margaret Farley understands as a "just love": "A love is right and good insofar as it aims to affirm truthfully the concrete reality of the beloved."[32]

Rather than embracing justice as a guiding value of sexuality, though, Christianity has promoted, throughout its history, an ethic that views sensuality as immoral and sex as sinful, unless it occurs within prescribed circumstances and for prescribed purposes. In *Making Love Just*, Marvin Ellison argues for a new understanding of Christian sexual ethics that reframes the tradition that has been profoundly steeped in sex-negativity and the association of sex with sin. He argues,

> Because religious traditions remain dynamic and meaningful only by staying open to cultural change, adapting to altered conditions, and revising their assumptions as warranted, a major overhaul of Christian sexual teaching is necessary insofar as the traditional Christian framework has been constructed on the basis of devaluing the body, women, and nonheterosexual persons. Above all, this tradition is weighted down by an underlying suspicion that pleasure is at odds with what is genuinely ethical.[33]

He proposes an ethic of justice-love as a Christian ethic that provides a contrasting perspective that takes a "pro-sex, feminist, and gay-affirming stance and offers a radically different ethical framework about sex and sexuality."[34]

Ellison defines "justice-love" as a social ethic understood as "mutual respect, commitment, and care and a fair sharing of power, for gay and nongay, marital and nonmarital relationships alike."[35] He proposes several values that should guide an ethical assessment of human sexuality:

---

32. Farley, *Just Love*, 200.

33. Ellison, *Making Love Just*, 24.

34. These ideas were first formulated in a 1991 Presbyterian study document, "Keeping Body and Soul Together: Sexuality, Spirituality, and Social Justice," of which he was a primary co-author. See Ellison, *Making Love Just*, 32–33. The ideas were also developed in Ellison's earlier work, *Erotic Justice*.

35. Ellison, *Making Love Just*, 21.

honoring the goodness of bodies and of sexuality; recognition of the diversities that are present in human experiences; concern for those who are sexually abused, exploited, and marginalized; accountability to the well-being of the whole community; learning from marginalized persons and communities.[36] These values shift the focus of sexual ethics away from an explicit judgment about types of relationships and moves it toward a judgment about the way in which relationships are grounded in mutuality, care for each other, and justice-love. According to Ellison: "This more encompassing sexual ethic redraws the boundaries between good and bad sex by sketching the normative value of justice-love as central to an ethically principled intimate relation."[37] A progressive Christian sexual ethic considers the moral qualities of justice, mutuality, trust, and respect exhibited in the relationship, rather than the specific form the relationship takes:

> Utilizing a progressive theological lens, the moral problematic is no longer the 'sin of sex,' but rather the eroticization of injustice and the misuse of power to exploit and harm self and others. A justice ethic of sexuality highlights the centrality of a responsible use of power, including erotic power, to enhance personal well-being and strengthen community ties of mutual respect and care across social categories.[38]

Thus, relationships based on justice-love as an ethical principle are properly judged according to their moral actions, rather than the gender identification of the persons in the relationship.

The ethical action of prioritizing justice-love subjects the truth-telling of disruptive coherence to an ethical accountability. Its moral judgments are based on the quality of the relationships that are present between the persons, rather than on the gender composition of those relationships. It ensures that just relationships and experiences are at the heart of the embodied testimony of the coming-out process.

Honoring communal relationships is a second value that supports a developing queer moral agency. This ethical value recalls, for example, the experience of my parents-in-laws living with my partner and me that I discussed in the first chapter. In that situation, to honor the communal relationships of family involved carefully and thoughtfully negotiating the communication of truth-telling in a way that respected histories, cultures,

36. Ellison, *Making Love Just*, 32–33.
37. Ellison, *Making Love Just*, 33.
38. Ellison, *Making Love Just*, 34.

and traditions, and at the same time, balanced those needs with the ethical necessity to live truthful lives.

Our humanity, inextricably social and communal, exists in a complex web of both individual and collective realities. Our lived experiences are particular in the ways in which we interact with social discourses of power—for example, the ways in which gender, race, and class intersect in our lives and create multiple interactions of our bodies with those discourses. The truth-telling of disruptive coherence acknowledges and respects the intersectionality of lived experiences of culture, ethnicity, family, religious traditions, social class, immigration status, able-bodiedness, race, gender, and other markers of marginalized difference. Respect for these contextual realities challenges queer persons to mix truth-telling with actions that will be effective in a particular context. Coming out as disruptive coherence honors the concrete needs of strategic necessity that characterize the complexity of truth-telling that cuts against the grain and troubles established ways of thinking and acting.

Disruptive coherence takes into account all of the factors that exist as part of our personal and social contexts, and, rather than demanding adherence to an abstract moral norm, considers contexts and relationships that are vital in negotiating and communicating truth-telling. With the ethical value of honoring communal relationships, the action of disruptive coherence remembers that truth-telling occurs within our webs of relationships to which we are ethically accountable.

What practices might support a developing queer moral agency? The ethical values of prioritizing justice-love and honoring communal relationships undergird at least two ethical practices that contribute to the development of disruptive coherence: *embracing erotic embodiment* and *interrogating discernment.*

As noted earlier in the earlier discussion of the erotic, *embracing erotic embodiment* seeks the sacred in sensuality. It is hard to underestimate the radical transgressiveness of that assertion, especially when it is placed in the context of a long history of Christian statements that see desire and pleasure as sinful. As Jordan states so clearly: "The suspicion of an impure pleasure is the most radical and comprehensive principle in Christian sexual ethics, the one with the greatest power to exclude acts, desires, and dispositions."[39] For this reason, it is important to infuse the

39. Jordan, *Ethics of Sex*, 156–57.

spiritual practices of queer lived experience with ethical practices that resist and counter an oppressive religious tradition.

Progressive theologians have worked in recent decades to challenge the sex-negativity of Christian traditions in order to articulate a more positive understanding of desire and pleasure.[40] For the purposes of this chapter, I want to reflect upon and imagine how spiritual and religious communities might live out these positive interpretations in their lives.

As an ethical practice, embracing erotic embodiment is related to the Christian practice of honoring the body.[41] From this theological perspective the body must be honored because the body is made in the divine image, and therefore, sacred. However, even though Christian traditions have believed in the dignity of the body, certain bodies have not always been honored: poor bodies, LGBTQI bodies, raced bodies, gendered bodies, bodies with disabilities. Therefore, it more accurately needs to be expressed as honoring *bodies*. Romanticizing what it means to have a body has no place in the ethical practice of embracing erotic embodiment. As an ethical practice, it interrogates ways in which religious discourses have not honored marginalized bodies and embraces the discourses of resistance that those bodies have created.[42] The ethical practice of embracing erotic embodiment interrogates the effects of the contexts of racism, gender and sexual normativities, cultural bias, and colonialism on those marginalized bodies.[43]

As theologians we need to imagine how the sensuous acts of bodies reveal ways to embrace erotic embodiment, thereby honoring bodies. For example, Marvin Ellison proposes "ethical eroticism" as a way to think about how to honor our sexual bodies in relation to others.[44] As another

40. Margaret Kamitsuka provides a helpful overview of the efforts of feminist, womanist, and queer theologians to develop more positive theological understandings of pleasure in Kamitsuka, "Sexual Pleasure." For other helpful resources, see Burrus and Keller, *Toward a Theology of Eros*; Jung et al., *Good Sex*; Kamitsuka, *Embrace of Eros*; Shults and Henriksen, *Saving Desire*.

41. See Paulsell, "Honoring the Body" and Paulsell, *Honoring the Body*.

42. See, for example, Douglas, *What's Faith Got to Do with It*; Douglas, "Black and Blues"; Copeland, "Body, Representation, and Black Religious Discourse"; Eisland, *Disabled God*; Hero, "Toward a Queer Theology of Flourishing"; Kwok, "Body and Pleasure in Postcoloniality."

43. See, for example, Douglas: *Sexuality and the Black Church*; Hopkins, "Construction of the Black Male Body"; Cannon, "Sexing Black Women"; Kwok, "Asian and Asian American Churches"; Althaus-Reid, "'Let Them Talk . . . !'"

44. Ellison, "Reimagining Good Sex," 245–61. For Ellison, a renewed Christian sexual

example, Robert Goss, imagining the recovery of sexual pleasure from within a creation-centered spirituality perspective, proposes reclaiming the idea of "love-making as blessed on the Christian Sabbath."[45] It is the work of imaginatively engaging the practices of Christian traditions to find how they might support embracing erotic embodiment that can revitalize understandings of the meaning of honoring all bodies.

How might the ethical practice of embracing erotic embodiment support coming out as the practice of truth-telling, as embodied testimony? It is a truism that, nonetheless, deserves remembering: Changing the understandings of two millennia of teaching that is ambivalent about bodies, and passes negative judgment about the erotic, will not occur quickly. It is a project that requires ongoing resistance and persistent challenge from both within institutions and traditions and from outside of them.

I am suggesting that an ethical practice of embracing erotic embodiment supports coming out as embodied testimony through making sacred the action of intellectual, affective, spiritual, and moral wrestling. Embracing erotic embodiment values not just the goodness of bodies, desires, and sexuality, but also embraces the ongoing process of wrestling—with God, religious traditions, those with whom we are in relationship, ourselves, our cultures. Embracing erotic embodiment shapes the ability to contend with disciplinary powers that undermine and thwart queer becoming-selfhood-in-relation. It forms power that contests openly against social discourses of power for the purpose of human freedom toward more inclusive diversity.

Coming out as the erotic ethical practice of truth-telling, as embodied testimony, thrives on the moral action of wrestling that can make space for the *grace of disruption*. As a moral action, wrestling, formed from an

---

ethic reimagines erotic power, transforming it from a dangerous force requiring control to an energy that is "an intrinsic, constitutive component of our humanness" and "our embodied sensuality and capacity for connection" (247). He articulates several values that are the basis for an ethical eroticism that "undergirds an ethic that is sex-affirming and respectful of erotic power as a moral resource" (251). These include the following: "to honor the goodness of the body, of bodily integrity or self-direction, of mutuality, and of fidelity" (250).

45. Goss, "Gay Erotic Spirituality," 210. The full quote states, "Very few Christians have ever heard clergy speak of love-making as blessed on the Christian Sabbath. When I speak to Christian groups about blessed sex on the Sabbath, it frequently triggers an erotophobic response from individuals who have experienced profound shame and guilt about their homosexual feelings. The recovery of Sabbath sexuality may prove to be a promising trajectory for overcoming sexual shame and guilt and reclaiming sexual experience as sacred and holy."

ethical practice of embracing erotic embodiment, can open religious and spiritual lives to the grace of disruption. Grounded in the values of justice-love and honoring communal relationships, disruption becomes a grace for communication and truth-telling. Through the moral action of wrestling, perspectives can be opened up and overturned to understand the excluded other with greater depth. The disruption caused from wrestling has the potential to destabilize exclusionary thinking and interrupt fixed ideas of normality that disregard marginalized groups.

Interrogating discernment engages the Christian practice of discernment in a way that seeks to disrupt its normalized understanding as an individualized engagement with God whereby wisdom arises only from disengaging the world and daily life. As an ethical practice it critically challenges spiritual discernment that is privatized and disconnected from the concerns of communities, in order to embrace actions that enact justice towards oneself and towards others. Interrogating discernment seeks to unmask spiritual discernment that ignores social contexts and their power relations. Interrogating discernment embraces the wisdom of bodies, communities, experiences in context, cultures, spiritual practices, and traditions in order to understand God's wisdom.

The Christian practice of discernment can be described as "the intentional practice by which a community or an individual seeks, recognizes, and intentionally takes part in the activity of God in concrete situations."[46] It has a long historical tradition in Christian communities with various understandings in specific historical contexts.[47] Henri Nouwen articulates several general aspects of discernment as a spiritual practice that provides a useful perspective for it as a building block of disruptive coherence. First, spiritual discernment is about seeing through the appearances of things to find a deeper meaning and God's active presence in our experiences: "Perceiving, seeing through, understanding, and being aware of God's presence are what is meant by discernment." Second, spiritual discernment is about being seen by God: "Once we are willing to see and be seen by God, we can look for signs of God's presence and guidance in every appearance presented to our senses. Discernment becomes a new way of seeing (and being seen) that results in divine revelation and direction." Finally, the purpose of spiritual discernment is to understand God's action in our lives and

---

46. Rogers, "Discernment," 105.

47. For a helpful historical overview of discernment in the Christian tradition, see McIntosh, *Discernment and Truth*.

the calling that is revealed: "The purpose of discernment is to know God's will, that is, to find, *accept*, and *affirm* the unique way in which God's love is manifest in our life." Nouwen makes clear that coming to understand God's will is an action of freedom that "has nothing to do with passive submission to an external divine power that imposes itself on us. It has everything to do with active waiting on a God who waits for us."[48]

Discernment as a spiritual practice is deeply connected to our responsible human freedom. It refers to the ability to know what action to take in our lives as a result of being in a deep engagement with God, with our becoming-selfhood-in-relation, and with others in the contexts, relationships, and communities of our lived experience. These contexts, relationships, and communities are not neutral; therefore, the process of discernment necessarily includes examining existing power relations and including that understanding in the process of decision-making. Discernment occurs in the everyday circumstances in which living occurs, not in a space removed from them.

Traditional Christianity from a Western perspective has made normative a notion of spirituality as disconnected from material life. In "We Drink from Our Own Wells: Discernment and Liberation," Henri Nouwen describes his awareness of the limitations of his traditional understanding of spirituality and discernment from his experiences with Gustavo Gutiérrez in Latin America. Through his engagement with Latin American liberation theology he came to see the ways in which his spirituality had been deeply individualistic, one that served the needs of persons with the privilege of time and opportunity to develop an inner sense of silence that was removed from the material struggles of daily life. He states, "What I learned from Gustavo was that liberating spirituality must be rooted in an active and reflective faith, not a passive, private, or privileged contemplative experience. And that spiritual discernment is not just an individual gift but part of the struggle of the people of God."[49]

Engaging discernment with the energy of disruptive coherence requires centering it in concrete lived experiences of particular bodies, which are grounded in specific intersectional contexts and engagements with power. When the practice of discernment is freed from a norm that demands a privatized disengagement from the world, discernment can open up to

48. Nouwen, *Discernment*, 5–8.

49. Nouwen, "We Drink from Our Own Wells," in *Discernment*, 172.

include the ways that God engages humans in the midst of the resistances and enactments of power in lived experience in an unjust world.

The ethical practice of interrogating discernment arises from spiritual experiences of finding and experiencing the wisdom of God and community in the midst of the materiality of living as it engages with discourses of power and the struggle for justice. Challenging traditional notions of spirituality, contextual theologians from communities on the margins have articulated spiritualities from those communities that are deeply engaged with seeing the holy in lived experience and, especially, in the struggle for justice.[50] Spiritual discernment that finds God in the midst of experiences of social power, resistance, and community struggles disrupts privatized experiences of the holy and centers discernment directly in the struggle for justice. Grounded in the ways that communities find life in the midst of resisting life-defeating forces of injustice, interrogating discernment can be an ethical practice that works for the creation of justice-love.

I am suggesting that an ethical practice of interrogating discernment supports coming out as embodied testimony through assisting one's capacity to perceive new and cohering insight about one's relation to God, selfhood, spiritual grounding, communities, cultures, and religious traditions. These insights help in the formation of convictions about our becoming-selfhood-in-relation and the ways in which these convictions might challenge normative notions of morality. Engaging the wisdom of God as we come to know it through our engagement with the intersectionality of lived experience and discourses of power, religious and spiritual traditions, communities, and cultures works to form becoming-selfhood-in-relation in all of its multiplicity and motion.

Coming out as the erotic ethical practice of truth-telling, as embodied testimony, thrives on the moral action of perceiving insight, which can make space for the *grace of coherence*. The cohesion is not the false wholeness and static unity of "oneness." Rather, the grace of cohesion provides linkages for all of the pieces of becoming-selfhood-in-relation to be brought to our engagements with others. It is the interdependent wholeness of multiplicity, not the singular wholeness of unified oneness. The grace of coherence can

50. See, for example, Gutiérrez, *We Drink from Our Own Wells*; Aponte, *Santo!*; Berrú-Davis, "Theologizing Popular Catholicism"; Hayes, *Forged in the Fiery Furnace*; Hayes, *No Crystal Stair*; Townes, *In a Blaze of Glory*; Battle, "Liberation"; Pak et al., *Singing the Lord's Song in a New Land*; Usog, "Women's Spirituality for Justice"; Flunder, *Where the Edge Gathers*.

help to form convictions that can ground our resistances to moral normativities that are disconnected from diverse human experiences.

Disruptive coherence, then, arises from the disruptive act of affirming
the sacredness of the erotic and the cohering act of critically discerning
God's movement in our embodied living in and through religious and spiritual traditions, communities and cultures, and contextual power relations.
Valuing justice-love and communal relationships, disruptive coherence
is formed from ethical practices that embrace the sacredness of sensuality and a contextually grounded spiritual discernment that is not divorced
from the messiness of lived experience and the struggles for justice.

Forming Convictions and Moral Discernment

The values of prioritizing justice-love and honoring communal relationships, and the ethical practices of embracing erotic embodiment and
interrogating discernment, connect to coming out as embodied truth-
telling in an important way: they shape the embodied actions that empower coming out in the nuances and complexities of everyday life. These
values and practices form moral convictions that empower embodied
truth-telling and responsible freedom gained through embracing the
wisdom of God's animating spirit in us, our body-knowledge, and our
communities and relationships.

There is an irony in talking about forming "convictions" in terms of
queer freedom and becoming-selfhood-in-relation. The term is used in a
legal sense to speak about officially charged guilt as a result of doing something wrong and illegal. This usage of conviction as guilt has been carried
out against LGBTQI persons, both historically and in the present, where
there are laws against queer acts. In some religious contexts convictions are
used as a way to indict such acts as immoral. Religion also uses the idea of
convictions, however, in a positive and empowering manner to indicate a
firmly held belief that is grounded in faith, such as for example, to declare
a conviction in God as steadfast in love. It is in this sense of conviction as
a firmly held stance of faith that it becomes a liberating resource for the
ethical practice of coming out as embodied testimony.

There is a deep connection between forming convictions and acting
out of conscience. Convictions are formed, in part, by engaging the profound awareness of what is good and right that we receive from God, and
that is shaped and influenced through religious and spiritual communities,

cultures, and relationships. While conviction and conscience are not synonymous, they are connected in a way that points to what Howard Thurman calls the "inward center," the crucial part of becoming-selfhood-in-relation that is decisive in persons.[51]

The topic of conscience, throughout history and to the present, is complex and wide-ranging, considering, for example, issues of virtue, character, judgment, knowledge (fully informed or poorly informed), and freedom. It demands an in-depth treatment that is beyond the scope of this present work. However, in a discussion about forming moral convictions that empower coming out as embodied truth-telling, it is useful to consider the connection of conviction and conscience to a sense of moral integrity. To speak of the need to honor the integrity of conscience is to speak about the moral requirement to live an honest and truthful life. One caution, though: integrity can mean, by one definition, a condition of stable, undivided wholeness. I do not believe that such a state is possible in the midst of the competing claims of ethical demands and the complexity of their implementation. In its meaning as honesty and steadfastness, integrity makes space for the ongoing process by which we come to live moral lives.

Coming to an integrity based in conviction and conscience arises through a process of moral discernment. Richard Gula understands that moral discernment is a spiritual and evaluative process that is fundamentally connected to a commitment to God. Discernment in its connection to morality is "the process of discovering the course of action most fitting to what our fundamental relationship with God demands."[52] In looking to make a moral decision in connection with religious faith, one needs to consider whether the action is the right action, but that action must also be consistent with a person's fundamental commitment to God. In his thinking it is imperative to make a faith-based moral decision in light of that primary relationship with God:

> As a people of faith, we want to know what God is requiring of us, not just what the law or conventional behavior requires. The work of conscience is to discover the call of God in each situation in order to know what God is asking of us in the here and now. Moral discernment, then, is something more than disciplined deliberation. It is a graced exercise of faith seeking to express itself in action.[53]

51. Thurman, *Jesus and the Disinherited*, 11.

52. Gula, *Moral Discernment*, 47.

53. Gula, *Moral Discernment*, 48.

Moral discernment and the integrity of its truth-telling, then, is profoundly connected to a spiritual sense of commitment to God's will in our lives. Moral integrity is a faithful becoming-selfhood-in-relation actively expressing its convictions for the work of justice.

There are stories from every community in which embodied testimony requires a deep moral discernment that grounds a steadfast commitment to the struggle for justice and human freedom. Martin Luther King Jr's "kitchen table prayer" is a profound example of an experience of moral discernment—one that fueled and sustained King's struggle against racism and segregation—that is often foundational in the long and difficult struggle against normative powers that maintain injustice.[54] For the purposes of this chapter I want to highlight briefly two such moral discernments from my own religious tradition that specifically focus on taking a stand in support of positive religious ministries for LGBTQI persons.

Jeannine Gramick, a Roman Catholic religious sister, is a co-founder of New Ways Ministry, a Catholic social justice and advocacy ministry in support of LGBTQI persons. In a chapter in which she explained her struggle with the Vatican and the controversies over her work in LGBTQI positive ministries, she used the metaphor of "God's shoes" to articulate her understanding of the role of conscience and moral discernment in her decisions and in her truth-telling about her work. She provides a helpful metaphor to explain moral discernment for embodied truth-telling that is grounded in a relationship and response to God's will. She speaks of the need to walk the journey of moral discernment in "God shoes," that is, the shoes that God asks us to walk in during life that represent our deep commitment to our fundamental relationship to God: "'finding our God shoes' is a poetic way of saying that we need to engage in the process of making an informed decision of conscience. If we are to grow in our faith and loving relationship with God, we must engage in moral discernment. Our God shoes require us to speak our truth."[55] Her metaphor of "God shoes" points to a moral discernment that is deeply related to her sense of connection to God and the demands of her conscience.

The work of John McNeill provides another story of moral discernment in the service of embodied truth-telling in support of the LGBTQI community. A Jesuit priest, he was challenged by the Vatican for his theological treatise, *The Church and the Homosexual* (1976), which critically

54. King, *Stride Toward Freedom*, 124–25.
55. Gramick, "God Shoes," 21.

examined existing church teachings on homosexuality, and for his work in ministries that supported and advocated for LGBTQI Catholics. After much controversy and struggle over two decades, he was expelled from the Jesuits because of his refusal to give up all public ministries for LGBTQI justice to which he felt called by God to continue. For him the decision was a struggle of conscience and moral discernment. He wrote to his superiors in the Jesuit community, "Whenever I pray over the possibility of obeying this order my spirit is troubled and I have a strong feeling that I do not have the right in conscience to abandon the gay community which has turned to me for help and guidance."[56] He felt morally compelled to respond to what he felt was God's call to serve LGBTQI Catholics. You could also say, as per Gula's point, that McNeill felt that he had to act in a way that honored his commitments of faith and his relationship to God.

The moral action of shaping convictions that are developed through engaging conscience and moral discernment can be used for the work of justice. It can open religious communities to greater inclusivity and acceptance of queer bodies, loves, and understandings of the divine. The formation of moral convictions can support and sustain the work of resisting and transgressing norms that exclude the queer responsible freedom.

Disruptive coherence—grounded in the values of prioritizing justice-love and honoring communal relationships and enacted in the ethical practices of embracing erotic embodiment and interrogating discernment—is moral formation that seeks to develop convictions that can empower the transgressive moral energies of disruption and coherence. Disruptive coherence can help to develop the spiritual maturity (that McNeill advocated) to trust in the authenticity of an engagement with God as we morally discern the decisions of coming out that require embodied testimony.

Concluding Thoughts

In this chapter I have tried to articulate two factors that develop the ideas of disruptive coherence. First, truth-telling connects to the erotic and, furthermore, the truth-telling of queer bodies and desires connects the erotic to coming out as a practice of embodied testimony.

Second, through engaging moral imagination, I sought to develop erotic ethical practices of truth-telling for disruptive coherence. In this

56. See Appendix Three, "A History of the Publication of This Book" in McNeill, *Church and the Homosexual*, 234.

section, I considered how disruptive coherence could be viewed as a moral formation that makes a more inclusive space for queer lives. I explored the values of justice-love and accountability to communal relationships as foundational to embodied testimony, and the ethical practices of embracing erotic embodiment and interrogating discernment as ways to enact those values. Finally, I discussed those values and ethical practices as embodied in forming moral convictions, and the role of conscience and moral discernment in shaping those convictions.

Coming out as disruptive coherence, as the erotic ethical practice of truth-telling, as embodied testimony, relies on the creation of moral convictions sufficient to create, support, and sustain transgression and resistance of the normativities of social discourses of power that compel compliance. Such convictions live and thrive in a spiritual connection to God that is found in lived experiences, spiritual and religious traditions, cultures, communities, and struggles for justice. As an ethical social practice that changes and develops as we change and develop, coming out as telling the truth about ourselves is a sacred praxis that binds us ever more to God, to each other and to all creation.

The question remains, though, about how this might actually be accomplished in the give-and-take messiness of conflicting demands and convictions that are too often a part of living. These are the questions of embracing disruptive coherence in lived experience to which we now turn.

_____ 5 _____

Embracing Disruptive Coherence

What does it cost to tell the truth?

I guess if your sense of self matches closely with the cultural grid of what you should mean, and you find those meanings pleasing, then the "truth" doesn't come too expensive. For the rest of us, though, it can cost a great deal.

—RIKI ANNE WILCHINS,
    "WHAT DOES IT COST TO TELL THE TRUTH?"[1]

G ender justice activist, Riki Anne Wilchins, wrote these words in 1993 as a specifically trans response to a question in Michel Foucault's writings in which he challenged a society's need to make a person's difference an object of study. Wilchins's answer to Foucault's question focuses on the need to understand the meanings that others ascribe to genderqueers as a matter of their survival: "The purpose of a gender regime is to regulate these meanings and to punish those who transgress them. In order to survive, to avoid the bashings, the job discrimination, and the street-corner humiliations, my friend will be forced to place herself as a site of *truth* to be mastered . . . She must know how others see her so she can know how to see herself; otherwise, she enters society at her peril."[2]

The idea of the cost of truth-telling, and the ways in which it effects some more negatively than others, focuses coming out as disruptive coherence within struggles for justice. As a result of social discourses of power and the structural inequities that it creates and perpetuates, the cost for coming out as an erotic ethical practice of truth-telling must be placed in context with the intersectional realities of living in an unjust society. The

1. Wilchins, "What Does It Cost to Tell the Truth," 551.
2. Wilchins, "What Does It Cost to Tell the Truth," 549.

dynamic and ongoing process of coming out, with its fluid movements of revelation and covering and its relationships to the continuing process of human growth and development, must occur within a thoughtful engagement with the contextual realities of prejudice and discrimination. Coming out as a practice of truth-telling must be focused on the ways in which the intersectional realities of lived experience become a fundamental aspect and driver of how to negotiate the practice within our relationships.

Understanding the cost of truth-telling in coming out is at the heart of negotiating the complexity of becoming-selfhood-in-relation within the contexts of queer lives—lives that must live in the intersectionality of all that is brought to human interactions. Our bodies, our loves, and our commitments can all be contested as a result of normative discourses that do not include the reality and effects of social difference, and may, in fact, condemn them. The action of coming out as disruptive coherence must hold in tension the experiences of intersectionality and its actual consequences with the moral demand to live truthful lives. It seeks to create the opportunity for moral discernment to become a part of negotiating the fluidity of disclosure and hiddenness.

In this chapter I want to consider with a critical eye some aspects of how disruptive coherence might be engaged in lived experience. In order to accomplish this, I want to reflect upon positive and negative understandings of both disruption and coherence, as well as the limits of coming out as disruptive coherence. Finally, I will place these considerations in conversation with an experience of queer clergy truth-telling in a Protestant Christian tradition.

To begin, though, I want to discuss a working definition of disruptive coherence. Gathering together the building blocks of disruptive coherence discussed in the last chapter, it can be provisionally defined as *a transgressive action of embodied truth-telling that is formed from moral convictions for the purpose of resisting normative discourses that perpetuate injustice.* These convictions are shaped from the values of justice-love and the honoring of communal relationships, and, also, the practices of embracing erotic embodiment and interrogating discernment. Coming out as disruptive coherence does not center its contesting action in the articulation of an identity; rather, it centers its contesting action on the ongoing practice of testimony that articulates something significant and authentic about a person—something that challenges and overturns normative discourse— that makes it more possible for them to live freely and with transparency in their becoming-selfhood-in-relation. Coming out as disruptive coherence is truth-telling for the purpose of personal, communal, and social justice.

Going forward I want to reflect critically on this working definition and what it might mean in queer living.

Interrogating Disruptive Coherence

This work assumes that both disruption and coherence are positive outcomes for the process of coming out. It is worth thinking critically, though, about the positives and negatives of that assumption. Disruption can be destructive in a way that destroys and creates damage without a purpose of creating justice. It can be used as a manipulation that seeks personal gain. Coherence can function problematically as a homogenizing and normalizing factor that limits freedom and social difference. Coming out as disruptive coherence, therefore, must be critiqued to ensure its relationship to the struggle for justice. Disruptive coherence ought to function in support of queer responsible freedom and an increasing inclusion of cultures, communities, and institutions for the purpose of justice (right relation).

In "The Disruption Machine: What the Gospel of Innovation Gets Wrong," Harvard historian Jill Lepore challenges the ways in which the language of disruption, designed initially as a theory about why businesses fail, has become an overarching goal and metaphor of contemporary global economy, spreading beyond that context to become a metaphor about how the world should be understood. She states,

> Disruptive innovation is a theory about why businesses fail. It's not more than that. It doesn't explain change. It's not a law of nature. It's an artifact of history, an idea, forged in time; it's the manufacture of a moment of upsetting and edgy uncertainty. Transfixed by change, it's blind to continuity. It makes a very poor prophet.[3]

Lepore's critique of disruption that becomes a controlling metaphor and determinism of action puts boundaries in understanding what disruptive theories are capable of doing. Her words contest a romanticized idea of disruption as an end in itself.

A *negative disruption* breaks apart established norms indiscriminately only for the purpose of destruction and without a sense of the interruption participating in the creation of just relationships on personal, communal,

---

3. Lepore, "Disruption Machine." See also, Goldstein, "Undoing of Disruption."

and social structural levels. A *constructive disruption* is one that seeks to overturn oppressive norms for the purpose of greater inclusion of socially marginalized persons and the fostering of justice and fairness.

What might a constructive disruption look like in regard to coming out as the practice of embodied truth-telling? One possibility can be found in Marvin Ellison's challenge of traditional marriage norms for the purpose of creating a broader understanding of sexual justice. In this work he speaks to religious communities as they attempt to engage the reality of sexual and gender-based differences. In "Marriage in a New Key," he draws upon the Protestant value of reformation. He argues for the need to continue the reforming impulse in order to think of sexuality and gender in more inclusive ways: "The reformation needed this time concerns sexual difference and sexual ethics because this tradition has fostered sexual injustice. Its relational ethic has been constructed on the basis of heterosexual exclusivism, the presumption that the only acceptable sexual expression is heterosexual, marital, and procreative."[4] For Ellison, contradicting "religiously sanctioned sexual oppression" must include a critique of established sex/gender paradigms and the development of a new ethical paradigm that "respects a diversity of human sexualities and places the focus not on identity, but on conduct and the character of relationships."[5] In calling for reforming ethical paradigms on marriage and sexuality, I see him calling for a constructive disruption of oppressive discourses of gender and sexuality for the purpose of justice.

Another example of constructive disruption can be seen in the work of Thelathia Nikki Young on black queer ethics and normative ideas of family. In *Black Queer Ethics, Family, and Philosophical Imagination*, she explores black queer moral agency in the construction of family that challenges normative discourses. She articulates three "moves" in black queer theorizing that "subvert/negate normative notions of family": disruption-irruption, creative resistance, and subversive-generative imagination.[6] From her study (she does not make essentialist claims for all black queer persons), she observes these practices as the ways that black queer people enact moral agency:

> Black queer people are moral agents who enact family in ways that are simultaneously disruptive to current familial norms in our

4. Ellison, "Marriage in a New Key," 407.
5. Ellison, "Marriage in a New Key," 407.
6. Young, *Black Queer Ethics*, 9.

society, creatively resistant to the disciplinary powers at work in those norms, and subversively generative and imaginative in relation to establishing new ways of being in relationship.[7]

As a result of their exclusion from established norms of family, black queer people respond in various ways to create norms that are inclusive of their lived experiences. For Young, the dynamic of disruption-irruption both critiques and reorients black queer understandings of family relationships to push against norms that exclude them and, also, envisions a "counter normalizing norm-creation" that engages moral imagination and moral agency.[8] From the perspective of black queer ethics, she concludes that human relationality, both in family and more generally, ought to include "an irreducible *interdependence* and *liberating support* of human potentiality" that can support our process of becoming as well as our participation in "divine creativity."[9] In constructing a black queer ethic I see her engaging in a constructive disruption of established norms of family kinship in order to articulate new norms that create a greater inclusivity of voices and experiences, thus, participating in the work of justice.

To speak of coherence in the context of queerness might sound contradictory. Queer theorizing interrupts discursive norms that serve to punish difference and seeks to be destabilizing of that which is considered "normal." As Nikki Sullivan states, to queer is "to make strange, to frustrate, to counteract, to delegitimize, to camp up—heteronormative knowledges and institutions, and the subjectivities and socialities that are (in)formed by them and that (in)form them."[10] Queering works to disturb and trouble a *controlling coherence* that represses and makes invisible difference and multiplicity as way to create a homogenized and false depiction of unity. An *inclusive coherence* makes space for the multiple aspects that make up our becoming-selfhood-in-relation, makes them visible, and holds them together in our lived experiences.

What might an inclusive coherence look like in regard to coming out as the practice of embodied truth-telling? One possibility comes from the field of pastoral theology. In "Braided Selves: Theological and Psychological Reflections on 'Core Selves,' Multiplicity, and the Sense of Cohesion," Pamela Cooper-White offers the metaphor of "braided selves" as a way

7. Young, *Black Queer Ethics*, 10.

8. Young, *Black Queer Ethics*, 58–61.

9. Young, *Black Queer Ethics*, 186.

10. Sullivan, *Critical Introduction to Queer Theory*, vi.

to think about coherence that embraces multiplicity and makes it visible. She examines the problematic notion of a "core self" that excludes "the inherent relationality and interdependence of persons" and "reinforces individualism and the belief that somewhere, 'deep down' inside a person, there is finally an insoluble unity."[11] With other relational therapists, she distinguishes between multiplicity "as normative fluidity, mutability, and diversity of the self" and fragmentation, "a pathological sense of being in pieces without any reliable cohesiveness or going-on-being," acknowledging the human subjective need for some type of anchor.[12] She sees the idea of a "core self" as valid, but "*only* if understood as an *aspect* of all one's subjectivities, and not as an actual, definitive, or central locus of identity, agency, and purpose."[13] Thus a person's sense of a "core self" changes and grows as one's interdependent subjectivities develop. She suggests the metaphor of the multiple self as a braid whose strength comes from the capacity to interweave the many aspects of personal subjectivities:

> I would now identify four strands that "hold" a sense of self together without erasing or undoing our multiplicity: 1) our bodies, 2) our relationships, 3) our spirituality; and 4) our embodied ethical practices. This four-fold braid is conceptualized not as a single straight line, but as a three-dimensional weaving or net-work. The web or net of threads, taken together, constitutes a "whole"—but a whole whose very coherence and binding power is made up of our multiple subjective experiences and states of being-in-relation.[14]

In the metaphor of "braided selves," I see an inclusive coherence that has the capacity to bring together the multiple experiences of our becoming-selfhood-in-relation and make them visibly part of our lived experience.

Another example of an inclusive coherence can be found in Rita Nakashima Brock's metaphor of "interstitial integrity." In "Cooking Without Recipes: Interstitial Integrity," she proposes this metaphor to talk about ways that many Asian Americans develop a cross-cultural consciousness that gathers together the multiplicities of their identifications and experiences into a cohesive sense of identity. She understands it as a "a complex, evolving process over time, captured in moments of self-awareness and self-acceptance—brief interludes of consciousness that appear within the

11. Cooper-White, "Braided Selves," 207.
12. Cooper-White, "Braided Selves," 207.
13. Cooper-White, "Braided Selves," 210.
14. Cooper-White, "Braided Selves," 214–15.

tossing turbulence of many people and places."[15] She takes the idea of interstitial from biology and its understanding of *interstitium*, the tissue that connects the organs to one another:

> Interstitial tissue lives inside things, distinct but inseparable from what would otherwise be disconnected. It is a channel of life in and out of things separated and different. It makes a living, pulsating unity, both many and one. Without interstitiality, parts of my life would wither and die, unnourished by the connected tissues of memory that constantly flow in and out of my consciousness. Interstitial integrity is how I improvise a self, recognizing the diverse cultures and experiences that have made me who I am.[16]

Using her lived experience as a Japanese, mixed-race woman, who is liberal Protestant and educated in US schools, she examines these influences to understand how living with interstitial integrity has assisted Asian American women to "find what is sacred by taking into our lives all that has touched us."[17] In the metaphor of interstitial integrity, I see an inclusive coherence that embraces the multiplicity inherent in lives and experiences and holds them together creatively to engage the ongoing growth and potentiality of becoming-selfhood-in-relation.

Disruptive coherence, as a moral formation of conscience, must resist engaging in a destructive disruption and a controlling coherence. As an erotic ethical practice of truth-telling, as embodied testimony, coming out as disruptive coherence must engage a constructive disruption and an inclusive coherence. It must both confront and search for developing new, more honest relationships. While the impact and effects of its transgressions can be difficult and painful, both to those who testify and those who receive it, its intention cannot be used as a bludgeon of change. Since coming out is an action rooted in our relationships as members of families, communities, religious traditions, and in a society with oppressive structures of injustice that marginalize, it ought to be negotiated within the complexity of those relationships with an ethical purpose that seeks to build right relations. As an act of political resistance for the purpose of justice it ought to occur within the social and personal contexts of communal relations and thus, requires truth-telling that is ethically centered and strategically focused for its effectiveness.

15. Brock, "Cooking Without Recipes," 126.
16. Brock, "Cooking Without Recipes," 126.
17. Brock, "Cooking Without Recipes," 140.

Coming out as an act of disruptive coherence overturns exclusive normativities that enforce and sustain gender and sexual injustice. It is an act of resistance that creates new norms that include diverse and marginalized experiences. Coming out as an act of embodied testimony, grounded in multiplicity and intersectionality, seeks to strengthen communal relationships through embracing that which is considered as Other. Its aim is to make ethical space for the varieties of human gender and sexual expression, and through that inclusion, create new norms that can reorient and redefine those discourses of power towards an ethic of sexual and gender justice.

Limits of Disruptive Coherence

Understanding coming out as a practice exposes it to some of the limits of practices. Most significantly, practices can become routinized and ritualized without critical thought, descending to the rigidity of "but that's not how it's done." Practices have power both in their creation and enactment and groups can reify these power relations. Also, because practices emphasize standards of excellence, they can become normalizing functions that blunt and tame their disruptive and transgressive energy. In short, practices, even ones that intend a constructive disruption and an inclusive coherence, run the risk of becoming domesticated and concerned with supporting justice only for specific persons at the expense of others whose lived experience is either invisible or less valued—and often both.

I want to discuss briefly two areas that I believe are important potential limitations that must be countered for coming out as disruptive coherence to sustain its radical, transformative, justice-seeking potential: assimilating difference and making coming out compulsory.

One of the dangers of seeking coherence in one's becoming-self-hood-in-relation, even as it is disruptive of certain normativities, lies in assimilating that difference, that is, its potential to be co-opted into existing unjust structures. The work of gender and sexual justice that ignores other forms of social injustice weakens the transgressive ethical practice of coming out as disruptive coherence. As an example, in the early 2000s Lisa Duggan coined the term "homonormativity" to depict a neo-liberal LGBT politics that, while advocating for gay inclusion, seeks assimilation into heteronormative structures and does not challenge them.[18] Such a

18. Duggan, "New Homonormativity."

stance does not confront existing oppressive structures of injustice and dominant discourses of power that exclude socially marginalized persons. A homonormative position has the capacity to dilute the disruptive transgressions of coming out through assimilating difference into existing cultural and economic normativities.[19] By removing it from the concerns of socially marginalized groups and the wider struggle for justice, assimilating difference into oppressive normativities undermines coming out as disruptive coherence.

Another limitation of coming out as a disruptive coherence, perhaps the most problematic, is the potential for making coming out compulsory. This is a complicated issue to consider because the danger of making coming out compulsory exists in the same conversation as the danger of living untruthful lives. It is exactly this location of complexity that coming out as an erotic ethical practice of truth-telling seeks to address. It embraces the intersectionality of lives and makes it an imperative aspect of action, making clear that social positionality affects where, when, and how truth-telling is communicated. It is the space of ethical judgments that negotiate the fluidity of being out and being in the closet, disclosure and hiddenness, revelation and covering. When the multiplicity of lives becomes a fundamental part of negotiating, when the contexts of race, gender, sexuality, class, bodies, and other markers of otherness are central components of moral reasoning, then the enactment of truth-telling becomes both disrupting and cohering.

Coming out cannot be compulsory because moral judgments are not rigidly fixed and immediately predictable. Judgments are made in real-time in response to the exigencies and competing claims of a situation that exists in the context of the ethical responsibility to live truthful lives. *Living truthful lives is an ethical mandate; moral judgment responds to the complexity of how to negotiate the communication of those truths.* For example, there are significant reasons of bodily safety, communal belonging, relationship stability, health status, and material necessity that make non-disclosure a needed aspect of queer living in particular contexts and for specified periods. As a process of becoming-selfhood-in-relation, coming out occurs over time as a dynamic energy of growth. Coming out as the erotic ethical practice of truth-telling participates in this growth—embodied testimony matures and changes as one's becoming-selfhood-in relation develops.

19. For an interesting discussion on this topic, see Clare, "'Finally, She's Accepted Herself!'"

Indeed, there are times when covering is necessary, and even desired in a particular context. However, covering comes with a cost that over time can be debilitating. Masks protect and can in moments be used strategically and subversively.[20] But masks are meant to be taken off. Making the mask permanent can significantly undermine one's ethical center. When faced with targeting as a result of the multiple identifications (some visible and some not visible) of many queer lives, covering may be a strategic necessity, but it is the role of moral judgment to weigh the costs and determine how they are negotiated in the real-time experiences of seeking to live truthful lives. The more significant the pressure of intersectionality, the greater the cost of coming out. Thus, as an ethical issue, making coming out compulsory, particularly in the context of the intersectionality of many queer lives and its consequences, violates the demands of justice by making truthtelling more costly for some than for others. In this way, making coming out compulsory undermines disruptive coherence.

The collision between intersectionality and practices of truth-telling are apparent in Kenji Yoshino's argument that the compulsory demand to cover social difference is the unfinished work of civil rights legislation. He uses covering in the sense of the necessity of those possessing stigmatized social difference to cover or veil those differences in order to avoid penalty from regulating powers. In *Covering: the Hidden Assault on Our Civil Rights*, Yoshino—a professor of constitutional law, Japanese American, and openly gay man—sees a parallel between the history of the LGBT civil rights struggle and his own journey to some sense of authenticity in his selfhood. He understands these movements to be society's compulsory demands over time for social conformity of minoritized persons, which were also present in his own struggle. In the demand for *conversion*, non-normative aspects of a person had to be eradicated, literally changed into conformity. Moving away from conversion demands, the compulsory demand became *passing*, the requirement not to change selfhood, but to make sure that one's selfhood remained a secret, with disclosure subject to serious disciplining. He believes that society has now moved to the compulsory demand of covering, that is, acceptance of many aspects of difference, but with a price

---

20. Su Yon Pak discusses the subversive use of masks in the Korean traditional mask dance (*tal-chum*). The subversive power lies in its capacity to be put on and removed. In the context of the spirituality of Korean-American adolescent girls and the prevalence of eyelid surgery, the eyelid surgery can be a permanent mask that loses this subversive power. See Pak, "I's Wide Shut."

attached: the demand to veil those stigmatized differences, often cultural, in order to participate in normative social structures and cultures.

Pertinent to the discussion on disruptive coherence and the danger of making coming out compulsory, he offers a useful perspective to consider. He distinguishes between a covering *performance* by those who are targeted because of difference, and a covering *demand* by those protected by dominant discourses. He states:

> I believe authenticity will look and feel different for each of us. I have elaborated my own gay identity by covering in some ways and flaunting in others, and will doubtless change that balance over time. I am not against all covering, but only against coerced covering. For this reason, I am much more likely to contest a covering *demand* by a homophobe than a covering *performance* by a gay individual . . . My real commitment is to autonomy—giving individuals the freedom to elaborate their authentic selves—rather than to a rigid notion of what constitutes an authentic gay identity.[21]

Yoshino's distinction makes clear the power and positionality issues that are present in the dynamics of covering. Because the necessity of covering relates to the needs of those who are marginalized, coming out as disruptive coherence prioritizes how relationships exist in relation to dominant power discourses as a factor in the negotiations of how, when, and where that truth-telling is communicated.

How might the limitations of disruptive coherence be mitigated? A critical awareness of the relationship of persons to social, communal, and societal power, and their relationship to privilege or marginalization as a result, undergirds an important assumption of coming out as embodied testimony: coming out reveals one's difference in the context of non-normativity and the cost that is born materially, communally, socially, and spiritually as a result of that non-normativity. Persons cannot "come out" into normative stances. The disclosures of coming out function to make stigmatized difference visible, and to create community that supports political acts to resist controlling normative discourses. Coming out as the erotic ethical practice of truth-telling overturns punishing and controlling regulatory discourses in order to make space for responsible freedom. Therefore, in order to mitigate the dangers of both assimilating difference and making coming out compulsory, the action of coming out as disruptive coherence must be situated in a socially marginalized location to dominant

21. Yoshino, *Covering*, 92–93.

discourses of power for the purpose of queer responsible freedom. It ought to be a justice-seeking action.

Disruptive Coherence in Praxis

As I have tried to suggest, the cost of truth-telling situates coming out as disruptive coherence in the intersectional reality of living. Embracing disruptive coherence, then, involves learning from examples of coming out experiences.

I have learned a great deal about embracing disruptive coherence from reflecting upon the experience of a small diverse group of clergy and candidates from the United Methodist Church who came out as a group in an action of truth-telling. Their action created a larger action of clergy in the denomination who also came out as LGBTQI. While they have not used the language of disruptive coherence, I found that their action, focused specifically on issues of discrimination toward LGBTQI clergy within their own church community, has aided my own critical reflection and attempts to develop disruptive coherence and coming out as an erotic ethical practice of truth-telling.

On May 1, 2016, a diverse group of fifteen clergy and candidates from the New York Annual Conference of the United Methodist Church (UMC) came out about their gender and sexual difference in an open letter to the people of the denomination.[22] They were explicitly challenging the legitimacy of a rule in the formal structure of the United Methodist Church that prohibits openly LGBTQI persons from ordination.[23] In this letter they acknowledged the ways that their region of the church had previously spoken out against the "denomination's prejudice and exclusion of LGBTQI people," allowing them some measure of safety and acceptance. Through their action, they sought to challenge the larger denomination's policy against LGBTQI persons and call out the targeting they have experienced as a result of those policies. The group makes clear that as a matter of justice they must challenge

22. See www.umqcc.org for information and documents related to their actions. I would like to thank the Reverend Lea Matthews, one of the original signers, for her information and insight about the case and her own experiences of its effects.

23. The rule in question states: "'The practice of homosexuality is incompatible with Christian teaching. Therefore, self-avowed practicing homosexuals are not to be certified as candidates, ordained as ministers, or appointed to serve in The United Methodist Church." See the following link from the United Methodist Church website: http://www.umc.org/what-we-believe/what-is-the-denominations-position-on-homosexuality.

a requirement that forces them to lie about themselves in a way that does moral violence to them and to others, communicating a false message that LGBTQI persons are damaged in their creation by God:

> We cannot hide in the welcome of our conference. We are com-
> pelled now to speak out and tell the whole truth of who we are
> to the wider church. Ministry requires honesty, courage, integrity
> . . . Yet the UMC demands that we not tell our truth about who
> we are in order to be in ministry. It requires us to pretend we can
> excise parts of ourselves that are LGBTQI, and to present a dis-
> torted version of ourselves to the world—all in order to avoid be-
> ing hunted down and kicked out for being 'self-avowed practicing
> homosexuals.' It does violence to our souls. It is the very opposite
> of the integrity that is foundational to ministry. This demand is
> fundamentally unjust, and we can no longer be complicit in up-
> holding and reinforcing it.[24]

They called on other LGBTQI United Methodist Church clergy to join them. They called on ordination boards to refuse to discriminate and to declare it openly, and they called on bishops of the United Methodist Church to refuse to process complaints against LGBTQI people. Finally, they called on all United Methodist Church members to refuse complicity and to protest the unjust rule at the denomination's annual meetings until the injustices to LGBTQI persons ends.

On May 9, 2016, prior to the denomination's General Conference, a second letter was issued to the members of the denomination. This letter consisted of the original fifteen who came out, along with over one hundred other United Methodist clergy who responded to the call (from the original letter) to join in the struggle and come out publicly themselves. After the document was released additional signatures were added, with a total of over 140 signatures. In this letter they talked about their covenant with the members of the United Methodist Church in baptism and in their call to ministry, which the community affirmed through their ordination. They challenged the rule against the ordination of openly LGBTQI persons in a way that was both personal and structural:

> while we have sought to remain faithful to our call and covenant,
> you have not always remained faithful to us. While you have

24. Reconciling Ministries Network, "Call to Declare 'We Are!' An Open Letter to the People of the United Methodist Church" in the United Methodist Queer Clergy Caucus (UMQCC) website: www.umqcc.org.

welcomed us as pastors, youth leaders, district superintendents, bishops, professors, missionaries, and other forms of religious service, you have required that we not bring our full selves to ministry, that we hide from view our sexual orientations and gender identities. As long as we did this, you gladly affirmed our gifts and graces . . . While some have been lucky to serve in places where we could serve honestly and openly, there are others in places far more hostile, who continue to serve faithfully even at tremendous cost to themselves, their families, and yes, even the communities they serve, who do not receive the fullness of their pastor's gifts because a core part must remain hidden.[25]

They explained that they decided to come out at this time to be clear that they seek to remain in relationship with the church and its people. They believe that, even if they were to be expelled, there will be other LGBTQI persons who will follow them into ministry: "You cannot legislate against God's call. The 'LGBTQI' issue is not one that can be resolved through restrictive legislation but instead by seeing that all persons are made in the image of God and welcomed into the community of faith." They also came out to support LGBTQI youth, and to remind them of God's love and care, in the face of condemnation they may hear at church, and to invite them to listen to God's calling for their place in the United Methodist Church.

At the end of the United Methodist Church's General Conference in 2016, the church made a decision to study the issue for two years and to come back to the community with some resolution to the issues that were raised. They established a globally diverse group of UMC clergy and lay persons, including LGBTQI members and clergy, representing the multiple theological and cultural perspectives that are in conflict over the issue, calling it, the Commission on a Way Forward.[26] As an important note, on October 26, 2016, after the commission participants were named, some members of the group who signed the original letters issued a statement of response. They challenged the insufficient representation of LGBTQI persons on the commission, as well as the lack of racial and gender diversity among the appointed LGBTQI participants.[27]

25. United Methodist Queer Clergy Caucus, "A Love Letter to Our Church from Your LGBTQI Religious Leaders": www.umqcc.org.

26. See the United Methodist Church website for more information about this commission: http://www.umc.org/who-we-are/commission-on-a-way-forward.

27. United Methodist Queer Clergy Caucus, "LGBTQI Clergy Respond to Naming of Special Commission," https://www.umqcc.org/lgbtqi-clergy-respond-to-naming-of-special-commission.

Those who signed the coming out documents established the United Methodist Queer Clergy Caucus, defining themselves as follows:

> The United Methodist Queer Clergy Caucus (UMQCC) is made up of lesbian, gay, bisexual, transgender, queer, and intersex people who are called, commissioned, and ordained clergy in the United Methodist Church.

> UMQCC seeks to act in solidarity with one another and others who have been marginalized in the church. Grounding ourselves in the call to Christian ministry, we strive to be an embodied prophetic witness of the church's future. We are agents of Christ's redemptive love in The United Methodist Church for the transformation of the world.[28]

With this statement, the group makes clear its connection beyond themselves to all of those who have experienced marginalization in their church community.

As of the writing of this text, the United Methodist Church is in the midst of the discussion process and, also, continues to struggle over the reality of LGBTQI clergy and the issues raised by the actions of the queer clergy.[29] For the purposes of this chapter, I would like to focus on the two letters that prompted the creation of the commission to understand what they might reveal about embracing disruptive coherence.

Reading through the documents on the UMQCC website, it is hard to miss what appears to be the heart of the matter that fueled their action: the desire (a) to reveal themselves as a moral action of conscience that sought to remove their complicity with a church discipline that forced them to lie about themselves, (b) to support other LGBTQI persons in the church, especially youth, and (c) to engage in that truth-telling for the purpose of justice for and inclusion of gender and sexual minoritized persons in the church.

In the previous chapter I talked about the values of prioritizing justice-love and honoring communal relationships, and the ethical practices of embracing erotic embodiment and interrogating discernment as fundamental components to developing disruptive coherence. Here I would

---

28. See the UMQCC website: https://www.umqcc.org/who-we-are.

29. For information about the ongoing struggles, see the Reconciling Ministries website: https://rmnetwork.org/news/umc-news/ and the UMQCC website: https://www.umqcc.org/jc-faq.

like to consider the ways in which these actions of coming out reflect these values and practices.

Both of the values of justice-love and honoring communal relationships are present in their actions. While there is no explicit discussion of justice-love in the letters, there is, however, a clear challenge to the official rules of the denomination that characterize their lives as "incompatible with Christian teaching." I see them arguing implicitly to be judged on the quality of their actions, rather than on their gender and sexual identifications. For example, in the May 1 letter they challenge the requirement that they hide themselves as "premised on a lie" that causes harm in its communication that there is something wrong in how God created them. This letter stands in solidarity with other UMC clergy who have previously faced charges, either publicly or quietly in their own churches, and were forced out of the ministry, seeking the same demands of justice for them. In the May 9 letter they remind the community of their common relationship through baptism and the approval of their call to ministry by the community. In both letters they implicitly challenge the community to affirm their leadership because of who they are and their calling by God, not because of their gender identity and sexual orientation.

They pointedly seek to remain in relationship with the community, while resisting the discrimination they feel should not be present in the church. The May 9 letter is explicit in this regard. They reply to those who tell them to simply leave the church saying, "Is leaving home ever that simple?" and then go on to explain the ways that they find their spiritual home uniquely in the United Methodist Church and Wesleyan spirituality. When explaining their reasons for coming out they state, "Foremost, we want you to know we still love you and seek to remain in close relationship with you." They also make a claim for the larger LGBTQI population in the church: "LGBTQI people and their families exist in every church in every continent of this denomination. They are seeking to remain faithful to you." In the May 1 letter they make a special point to make clear that they value and respect the ways that their New York regional group has supported them and has fought for justice for the LGBTQI community both in the church and in the wider society.

In what ways has their action engaged the ethical practices of disruptive coherence? It is more difficult to see these practices overtly, but I find threads, at times visible and at times less visible, of the ethical practices in their actions that point to possible motivations behind the statements. For example, in refusing to hide a significant aspect of their bodily enactment in the world and their family relationships, they are embracing erotic embodiment. In the May 9 letter they point to the cost of hiddenness for them, their families, and their communities because "a core part must remain hidden." When voicing their support of LGBTQI youth they implicitly are valuing queer bodies and queer loving, noting: "These young people are more at risk for suicide than their peers, in part, because of the condemnation they hear from pulpits and pews of their churches."

Threads of interrogating discernment can be found in the way in which they indicate the contradictions present in the reality of their experiences and the judgments against them. For example, in the May 1 letter they indicate the contradiction between the actions they perform as ministers and the requirement to hide themselves: "Ministry requires honesty, courage, integrity. We teach our Sunday school children to speak the truth. We challenge our congregations to see Jesus in 'the least of these.' We mirror God's welcome at our communion table. Yet the UMC demands that we not tell our truth about who we are in order to be in ministry." In the May 9 letter they speak about the contradiction between the fact that they have been accepted as leaders to do the work of the church, but only if they remained hidden as LGBTQI persons: "While you welcomed us . . . [for] religious service, you have required that we not bring our full selves to ministry, that we hide from view our sexual orientations and gender identities. As long as we did this, you gladly affirmed our gifts and graces and used us to make disciples of Jesus Christ for the transformation of the world in the varied places that you sent us." These instances indicate a spiritual discernment that is deeply rooted in their experiences as LGBTQI Christians.

I find important learning for embracing disruptive coherence in this example of queer coming out. Their resistance as a group seems to have made an important difference in their capacity to be strategically effective in challenging the community. The truth-telling of coming out is most typically depicted as an independent action that one takes alone. Clearly, in the case of engaging with family or personal relationships, the ability to communicate individually is often needed in order to establish new ways of relating that incorporate the newly visible aspect of becoming-selfhood-in-relation. But, coming out as embodied testimony, whether in a group or individually, makes clear the interdependence of the process. Queer coming out as truth-telling arises within communities of relationships and extends to the new ones entered. More significantly, the interdependence of relations and the supports they develop can assist in negotiating the risks that intersectionality presents. In both letters they make clear that some LGBTQI clergy are less targeted, and others serve in locations with hostility that targets them to an even greater degree. Functioning as a group, their resistance to the rule of the governance structure created the possibility of support for members who were negotiating other discourses of power in addition to one of gender and sexuality. Their truth-telling as a group made space for others to join in that truth-telling. One learning, then, might be the fundamental necessity of personal, communal, and institutional supports for embodied testimony.

A second learning arises from the group's strategic intention to engage in their truth-telling to coincide with the church community's General Conference, which is the global meeting of the United Methodist Church held every four years. This relates their action to another practice in Christian communities—the practice of how a community organizes itself. Larry Rasmussen refers to this practice as "the shaping of communities":

> The shaping of communities is the practice by which we agree to be reliable personally and organizationally. This practice takes on life through roles and rituals, laws and agreements—indeed, through the whole assortment of shared commitments and institutional arrangements that order common life.[30]

For Rasmussen, shaping communities functions as the "choreography" of all the other practices of a community.

By challenging a law that discriminated against LGBTQI clergy at the community's General Conference, they were engaging in the practice of testimony in the context of the practice of the shaping of the community. This was politically strategic in that it made use of an existing church structure that could create ways to change the discriminatory law. It also made clear their desire to challenge the law as members of the community in a struggle for justice. In effect, they were using a practice (testimony) to disrupt an unjust norm through the vehicle of another practice (shaping communities) as a way to both honor the relationships in which they belonged and engage a struggle for justice. Another learning, then, might be the usefulness of employing embodied testimony within the context of other community practices.

---

30. Rasmussen, "Shaping Communities," 118.

A final learning arises from the basic stance of their truth-telling—that they refused to live a life based on lies and they no longer wanted to be complicit in the lying that was required of them in order to serve the community. This point goes back to Yoshino's helpful distinction between a covering demand of a discourse of power and a covering performance of a targeted person. In this case they seemed to be saying that they resist the covering demand (and, likely, in some instances, a passing demand) as unjust and do not want to be complicit in it. They also seem to be saying that they have used a covering performance as protection, but at a cost to themselves, their families, and the communities they serve. In this way they indicate that their truth-telling empowered them in their resistance. A final learning, then, might be the role of coming out as an erotic ethical practice of truth-telling for enhancing queer freedom and power.

Concluding Thoughts

In this chapter I have sought to critically reflect upon the engagement of disruptive coherence in lived experience and in struggles for justice. First, through interrogating disruptive coherence I distinguished between intentions of disruption that are negative and controlling and intentions of coherence that are constructive and inclusive. As an action of moral formation of conscience, disruptive coherence seeks a constructive disruption whose purpose is the creation of justice and an inclusive coherence whose purpose is to include the multiplicities of human identifications. Next, I examined the limitations of disruptive coherence, clarifying the danger of its potential to assimilate difference into normative unjust structures and its potential to make coming out compulsory. Finally, I considered how disruptive coherence might be operative in the coming-out experiences of LGBTQI Christian clergy in the United Methodist Church, and what learning might be present in that experience for the development of coming out as an erotic ethical practice of truth-telling.

The question of the cost of truth-telling, and for whom, remains present as I continue developing my thinking. I am left now with a core question at the heart of embracing disruptive coherence: What empowers the courage to take the risk of coming out as a practice of embodied truth-telling? Is it the support of community, family, or tradition? Is it social norms? Anger? Desire? Likely it is all of these, and perhaps more. On a deep level, though, the courage to take such risks of truth-telling are a function of God's grace and God's calling in our lives.

A spiritual awareness of calling in the practice of truth-telling can connect us to the ongoing journey of becoming-selfhood-in-relation. This dynamic movement of becoming can be seen in Justin Tanis's understanding of calling: "Calling is about what we are to *do* and about who we are to *be*, as well as who we will *become*."[31] In his own life he views gender as a calling, a journey that is part of his becoming: "I was called to trust God and step out into uncharted territory to learn about myself and about who and what God has called me to be."[32] In our spiritual and moral discernment, queer persons can come to understand the relationship between our becoming-selfhood-in-relation and what must be done to participate in the creation of a just world. It is the sacred work of an ongoing embracing of disruptive coherence.

31. Tanis, *Trans-Gendered*, 146.
32. Tanis, *Trans-Gendered*, 146.

6

Coming Out as a Transformative Practice

*T*he coming out action in the United Methodist Church that I discussed in the last chapter is an example of disruptive coherence in practice. Their resistance to a coerced invisibility or, in some cases, a slightly visible presence that goes unacknowledged was both a demand for justice and an impetus to the community to expand its understanding of inclusion.

This leads me to a question that I want to pose as both a conclusion and as challenge for imagining next steps: How might coming out as disruptive coherence be a transformative practice for justice to create more diverse and inclusive Christian communities?

Coming out as disruptive coherence can be an ethical practice of (a) acknowledging and making visible bodies and perspectives that are marginalized and invisible, and (b) embracing and including those disregarded bodies and perspectives in the creation of just communities. Coming out as disruptive coherence, then, can be a *transformative ethical practice of acknowledging and embracing the marginalized and disregarded in the work of justice.* The work of acknowledging and embracing is intended to be understood as critical actions of resistance to discourses of power that limit responsible freedom, and proactive creations of new visions, possibilities, and strategies for enacting more diverse and inclusive communities. Acknowledging seeks to make visible what is left out and embracing seeks to include what has been excluded.

What might disruptive coherence as the work of acknowledging and embracing the marginalized and disregarded look like in praxis? In the remainder of this chapter I envision two basepoints that could serve as a grounding for its concrete praxis. With a focus on Christian communities in practice, I sketch them out with the intent to imagine new possibilities for coming out as disruptive coherence to be a transformative practice for justice.

Envisioning Disruptive Coherence and Justice

The first vision for a concrete praxis of acknowledging and embracing the marginalized and disregarded is to *create opportunities in communities to profess one's moral conviction of counter-normativity and challenge its exclusion*. By this I mean concretely developing rituals, practices, and communal occasions that have structured chances to own publicly one's *difference* and push back against the discourses that regulate its visibility. In religious communities, practices exist to affirm one's acceptance and belief in communal norms. I am envisioning a structured role for dissent that is based on moral convictions for the purpose of the work of justice.

Using the word "profess" to challenge injustice might sound slightly odd to contemporary ears in its formality. At the same time, it exists commonly in mainstream ideas of romanticized love—to profess undying love, to openly proclaim it is a staple of the love stories of popular culture. I use the word profess intentionally here to call forth its more radical meaning for use in the struggle for justice: to affirm a belief, to make a public affirmation of that belief, and to avow a commitment to it. In this meaning it points to the practice of testimony. To profess belief in God, in the Holy, in an awareness of transcendence in the world, is a profound commitment involved in living a spiritual life and participating in religious traditions. To use professing to affirm a moral conviction of one's principled difference from communal norms calls forth a more transgressive meaning.

Profession also has deep connections to confession. In some meanings professing and confessing characterize the same actions: to acknowledge belief or faith in someone or something. For example, a creed of a religious tradition is a statement of confession, an avowal of a particular belief. On a collective level, a confession comprises a community of believers who adhere to a specific list of creedal statements. More typically, however, confession refers to a disclosure or admission of something stigmatized, problematic, immoral, or illegal and is connected to a sense of shame and feelings of guilt. In this sense it is more connected to discourses and institutional structures of law and religion that compel admission of a truth about deviation from community norms.

These two meanings of confession—as an assertion of belief and as an assertion of guilt—ground a vision of professing a counter-normativity in a community. In my queer reading of this dynamic, the traditional meanings of belief and guilt become destabilized: one professes a discerned moral conviction that is counter-normative and seeks to move beyond guilt felt for an authentic expression of becoming-selfhood-in-relation. Professing is a truth-telling of a moral conviction about one's human freedom to live a non-normative becoming-selfhood-in-relation. The act of professing one's becoming-selfhood-in-relation challenges the exclusion of counter-normativities in the familial, communal, institutional, or societal worlds in which we engage. It pushes those relationships to engage the disruption of difference in their midst, wrestle with it honestly, and find ways to not only welcome it, but include it in their ongoing understanding of their identities.

A return to the thought of Michel Foucault—specifically his understanding of the definitions of confession as both assertion of belief and admission of guilt—provides a useful perspective to consider in discussions of truth-telling, confessing, and professing.[1] As noted in an earlier chapter, in *The History of Sexuality, Volume 1*, he makes important critiques about the use of confessing over the history of Western culture in many social discourses of power (religion, psychotherapy, law) to compel admission of the "truth" about sexual desires and actions that were defined by normative structures as deviant and to punish those transgressions.[2] This forced truth-telling created the discourse of "sexuality." A normalizing effect of the habit of confessing and the disciplining discourse of sexuality was at work in the compunction to admit the "truth" of sexual activity beyond the defined normativities. As Taylor states:

> For Foucault, this is how discipline works: first, a practice is forced on you, but if you repeat it enough times it becomes a habit, and eventually a habit becomes a desire. At this point, one ceases to see the practice one desires as an effect of power.[3]

1. Mark Jordan states, "Foucault repeatedly distinguishes two meanings of 'confession' in Christianity: the confession of faith and the confession of who one is, of one's state. These two are relatively autonomous and sometimes opposed. To declare true doctrine is not the same as to discover and express the truth about oneself. The two imperatives play back and forth across Christian history. Foucault is more interested in subdividing the second form of confession." Jordan, *Convulsing Bodies*, 135.

2. Foucault, *History of Sexuality, Volume 1*, 17–35.

3. Taylor, *Routledge Guidebook*, 22.

Thus, as a disciplining discourse of control, confessing the "truth" of sexual sin and "deviant" desires became a required function in response to the prescriptive demands of discourses of power that defined "normal" sexual relations.

In the last years before his death, Foucault changed this understanding of confession as a coerced truth whose function is to maintain the regulatory discourses that prescribe behavior. He began to think more intensively about confession in the sense of the articulation of a truth about oneself.[4] In this regard, he considers truth-telling practices directly through examining *parrhesia* (frank-speech).[5] Muers describes Foucault's understanding of *parrhesia* as "The risky action of one who calls the governing authority to account—from a position of relative powerlessness, and in a way that transgresses existing 'codes' of speech both in terms of what may be said and in terms of who is expected to speak and be heard."[6] A person engaged in frank-speech critiques the exercise of power as it normatively operates, with a sense of duty or obligation to do so.

Foucault outlines several essential characteristics of *parrhesia*.[7] First, a person engaged in frank-speech "tells all," but not in a negative sense of "chattering," rather it is a positive sense of telling the truth plainly without concealment: "telling the truth without hiding any part of it, without hiding it behind anything." Second, frank-speech is genuinely the personal opinion of the one speaking, and, furthermore, the person speaking must own those words which are binding to the person. Third, because it is based in the reality of a "fundamental bond" with the person to whom one is speaking, frank-speech involves risk. One risks possible damage to the relationship with the person to whom the speech is directed. Personal danger to the self is also a risk. Finally, because of the risks associated with engaging in frank-speech, one needs courage to undertake it. As Foucault states, "In

4. Judith Butler states, "In the last years of his life, Foucault returned to the question of confession, reversing his earlier critique in the first volume of *The History of Sexuality* . . . he rewrote his earlier position, finding that confession compels a 'manifestation' of the self that does not have to correspond to some putative inner truth, and whose constitutive appearance is *not* to be construed as mere illusion." Butler, *Giving an Account of Oneself*, 112.

5. The truth-telling practice of *parrhesia* is an aspect of Foucault's examination of "care for the self" and the "technologies of the self" that that are beyond the scope of this project. For more information, see Foucault, *Ethics*, 87–92 and 223–51.

6. Muers, *Testimony*, 87.

7. Foucault, *Courage of Truth*, 9–12. See also, Foucault, *Government of Self and Others*, 66–67.

a way, the parrhesiast always risks undermining that relationship which is the condition of possibility of his discourse."

Foucault's ideas about *parrhesia* are pertinent to the vision of creating opportunities in communities to profess one's moral conviction of counter-normativity as a way of acknowledging and embracing the marginalized and disregarded in the work of justice. His understanding of *parrhesia* can be useful to religious communities in its connections to professing. The characteristics of frank-speech relate to the spirit of what it means to profess: to speak truthfully and plainly without evasion, to own that truth as a moral conviction, to risk loss or danger to self in order to speak truth, and to have the courage to risk the loss. Muers crystalizes the characteristics of *parrhesia* in a way that connects it to professing in the queer meaning that I am exploring: "truthful speech that evades or challenges a particular structure of power, that refuses to say what is expected and instead says what needs to be said."[8] *Parrhesia* can be a powerful tool in one's attempt to profess a moral conviction of counter-normativity in a community.

How might Christian communities create a culture in which frank-speech and professing difference is a value? Creating a culture in the community that accepts difference and can handle constructive conflict helps to make a fertile ground for the creation of opportunities to profess one's difference. This task lands directly in the work of the community's leaders, both lay and ordained. Effective leadership can assist religious communities with resources to engage and successfully negotiate the disruptions of professing difference.

Emile Townes provides an example of the characteristics of leadership and truth-telling from the perspective of a womanist ethics of justice. She pairs pastoral action with prophetic action as a way to articulate effective ethical leadership in religious communities. She states that womanist ethics develops two "voices"—the pastoral and the prophetic—in order to be responsive to the needs of communities in both "the mundane and the extraordinary" in human lives and in the witness and work of religious communities.[9] The pastoral voice is a voice of community leadership that encompasses "the ability to be self-critical, to provide comfort, to accept others, and to encourage growth and change."[10] The pastoral voice hears the concerns of various persons and constituencies, seeks to be open to

8. Muers, *Testimony*, 94.

9. Townes, "Ethics as an Art," 42.

10. Townes, "Ethics as an Art," 42.

new information, accepts human frailties and limitations, and promotes transformations, both personal and institutional, that lead toward a faithful witness for the community. Its partner, the prophetic voice is one that resists injustice and engages in truth-telling: "Passion for justice and ethical witness has within it a concern for right relationships among peoples. We must have a strong and willful prophetic voice in response to the injustices we see heaped on people and the rest of creation."[11]

The pastoral and prophetic voice of leadership can be effective in creating opportunities for professing difference and negotiating its disruptions. The pastoral voice supports those who profess their non-normativity as well as those for whom that difference might be threatening. The prophetic voice pushes forward the demands of the excluded and seeks resolution that creates a more just community. Both voices can be used in embracing the moral action of wrestling and making space for the grace of disruption.

There exists a danger in an uncritical and naïve acceptance of professing that mistakes it as any form of protest or dissent from communal norms. As a statement of moral conviction, professing difference should be linked intentionally to a person's or group's spiritual discernment and moral integrity at a deep level that is authentic to themselves. The degree of personal danger and risk of loss at stake helps to determine the intent of professing difference. It is important, therefore, to distinguish between professing difference as a prophetic action for justice and protest that is simply posturing with an intention to mislead or manipulate. Professing difference ought to be an action of conscience and conviction.

In conclusion, disruptive coherence that creates opportunities to profess one's moral conviction of counter-normativity and challenges its exclusion in community is necessary in the work of justice. Making space for disruption, even welcoming it through rituals, practices, and communal occasions creates the possibility to own publicly a person's or a group's deviation from the communal norm and to challenge its exclusion. In this way, disruption becomes the sacred work of acknowledging and embracing the marginalized and disregarded.

Envisioning Disruptive Coherence in the Intersections

The second vision for a concrete praxis of acknowledging and embracing the marginalized and disregarded is to *create communities that welcome and*

11. Townes, "Ethics as an Art," 43–44.

include multiple identifications of becoming-selfhood-in-relation. In contrast to the first vison, which on first sight seems apparent that conflict will be part of it, this vision will be easier in the saying than in the doing. The distance between the ideal and the real—and the conflict that often accompanies the desire to welcome and include differences—challenges living out this vision. This represents the hard work of coherence, of pulling together the multiplicities of values, identifications, experiences, and perspectives in the creation of just and inclusive communities.

The ministry of Bishop Yvette Flunder at the City of Refuge United Church of Christ, a community founded and developed specifically with the aim of inclusion and acceptance of those who have been excluded from mainstream churches,[12] provides an important example of how Christian communities might embrace a radical inclusion of difference at the margins. She rejects theologies that understand religious communities as internally focused social clubs and challenges communities to look outward to include all persons, especially those who have been traditionally not welcomed or expelled from those communities. In *Where the Edge Gathers: Building Communities of Radical Inclusion,* she believes that as a result of a history of racism and cultural oppression religious communities with a history of rejection can in turn exclude others. She names this reality "oppression sickness" and challenges her own historical African American Christian church tradition for "marginalizing certain segments of society."[13] She argues for a church community of radical inclusivity that celebrates and embraces marginalized persons and groups:

> True community—true church—comes when marginalized people take back the right to fully "be." A people must be encouraged to celebrate not in spite of who they are, but because of who their Creator has made them. The balm that heals oppression sickness is the creation of accountable, responsible, visible, celebrating

12. The church describes its history in the following way: "The seed for City of Refuge UCC grew from a small group of mostly gay and lesbians Christians' deep desire to have a worship space that resembled the churches of their youth, but contained none of the toxic theology that was so often present in those spaces. Specifically the group desired a church that would (i) not be adverse to female clergy; (ii) welcome same-gender-loving and transgendered people; (iii) take seriously Jesus' commitment to social justice; (iv) value and welcome all people regardless of their race or social status; and (v) and be accountable to its members." See their website: http://www.cityofrefugeucc.org/our-history.html.

13. Flunder, *Where the Edge Gathers,* xiii.

communities on the margin of mainline church and dominant society.[14]

Such a community must be deeply grounded in the cultures of its members that are excluded in mainstream society and focused on efforts to interrupt and upend existing theologies in the tradition that exclude them.

In order to sustain a ministry of comprehensive acceptance, she proposes a "radical inclusivity model," a list of working assumptions that can assist Christian faith communities in their efforts to "create, sustain, and celebrate communities on the margins."[15] These include the following twelve steps:

- Step one begins with a basepoint: "Radical inclusivity is and must be radical." It demands that the community "reach out to the farthest margin, intentionally, to give a clear message of welcome to everyone."

- In step two, a radical inclusivity "recognizes, values, loves, and celebrates people on the margin," recalling the ways that Jesus was on the margins.

- Step three "recognizes the harm done in the name of God." It faces squarely the injury that has been done to persons who have been rejected by their communities.

- Step four understands that a radical inclusivity "is intentional and creates ministry on the margin" and "practices and celebrates the Christian community outside of the dominant culture."

- In step five, the primary goal of radical inclusivity is "not to imitate the mainline church." It is ministry rooted in "restoration," whereby the church seeks to "model and demonstrate the radically inclusive love of Jesus Christ."

- Step six proposes that radical inclusivity "requires a new way of seeing and a new way of being."

- In step seven, radical inclusivity "requires awareness, information, and understanding" to do the hard work of reexamining the community's relational ethics, develop a theology of radical inclusivity, and "destigmatize its view of any group of people."

---

14. Flunder, *Where the Edge Gathers*, xiv.
15. Flunder, *Where the Edge Gathers*, 134.

- Step eight asserts, "Radical inclusivity does not hide and works to undo shame and fear." This step challenges marginalized persons to develop community through a process of taking risk to be visible and celebrating their difference.

- In step nine, radical inclusivity "recognizes diversity on the margins." It recognizes intersectionality as a reality of marginalized persons.

- Step ten asserts that radical inclusivity "must be linked to preaching and teaching" that "defines, reinforces, and supports the collective theology of the community."

- Step eleven asserts that "inclusivity demands hospitality" and "acknowledges the fact that everyone already has a seat at the welcome table of God."

- The final step states that "Radical inclusivity is best sustained and celebrated when everyone in the community is responsible and accountable." It requires an intentional effort to design an inclusive framework for all to be welcome in the community. All members must be accountable to the welfare of the community.[16]

This model is useful for what it teaches about creating communities that seek to include multiple identifications of becoming-selfhood-in-relation. The work is rigorous, demanding, and grace-filled. It intentionally reaches out to the most socially marginalized persons and deeply values them. It seeks to promote justice, not charity. It shows pastoral care to those persons who have been hurt by exclusion from their religious communities for their difference. It is intentionally counter-normative and seeks to live a Christianity that embraces Jesus' radical inclusivity. It demands a transformation of one's views and engages those who are considered as Other in society, requiring examination of biases and prejudices. It sees the diversity of experiences and the multiple identifications of marginalized persons and groups. It is structured into the community as a part of the church's preaching and teaching. It demands hospitality to all and accountability of all to the work of the community. Flunder's vision of radical inclusivity represents an embodied testimony to the larger Christian community of the power and promise of welcoming and including the marginalized and disregarded.

16. Flunder, *Where the Edge Gathers*, 134–37.

As another way to think about creating radically inclusive communities, we can ask questions of how coming out as disruptive coherence can be used to build communities that welcome and include multiple identifications of becoming-selfhood-in-relation. Intersectionality complicates and interrogates LGBTQI experiences of coming out to make clear that gender and sexuality are not the only ways that marginalized groups have challenged their exclusion in Christian communities. Challenging racism, for example, has been an ongoing and historically significant reality. The language of coming out is connected to gender and sexuality identifications in particular and contextually specific ways. At the same time, persons who resist the passing and covering demands of stigmatizing normative discourses sometimes find coming out as a helpful metaphor as well. Understanding coming out as an embodied ethical practice of truth-telling might be useful in creating more space for the multiple marginalized identifications, both visible and invisible, that people bring into the religious communities. For example, persons with disabilities, persons who are abuse survivors or in recovery from substance abuse, formerly incarcerated persons, and persons from marginalized or targeted religious communities might find coming out as disruptive coherence to be a useful ethical practice for their own truth-telling.

It is important to note that groups find their own language to communicate their experiences, and the language of coming out as disruptive coherence might not be helpful or effective for them. I do not intend with this idea to create a normative discourse for all. I merely suggest it as an indication of my belief that practices of embodied truth-telling and of frank-speech might have significance in many aspects of intersectional realities of lived experience.

Monica Coleman's *Bipolar Faith: A Black Woman's Journey with Depression and Faith* is a powerful example of an experience of embodied testimony and frank-speech that both destabilizes and creates new coherences in herself and in community. Her memoir touches on the many overlapping identifications and marginalization in her experience dealing with, among others, racism, domestic violence, sexual assault, and mental illness, both her own diagnosed bipolar II disorder and a family legacy of depression and suicide. While she does not use the language of coming out, I read in her work practices of embodied testimony and disruptive coherence that call out for the creation of inclusive communities that have the ability to embrace multiple and intersectional lived experiences.

I was struck by several instances in her story that stood out to me as examples of professing—the power of the practice of embodied testimony, the conflicts of its disruptions, the reconstituting of its coherences, and the redemptive energy from the process of living them out.

In a reflection about her need during high school to "mask"[17] her emotional struggles and painful home life, she talks about the need to tell the truth to her parents about her unhappiness and the cost to her of the truth not being received:

> A middle place. Between truth and lies. Lying had become part of my life. I lied about loving my father. I lied about being happy. I lied about the harmony of my household. I lied with silences and masks. It was cultural, psychological, and domestic habit. It was how I stayed alive. But I always wanted to tell the truth. I wanted people to know. I wanted to be free to say it. But depression plays tricks with your mind. So does fear. It would take years for me to know that my happiness was as honest as my despair, and that the mask was as honest as my soul.[18]

In this instance, her convictions and frank-speech made visible to her parents her feelings of rage at her father's abusive behaviors and her deep emotional suffering, but they were not able to respond in a way that could embrace her truth-telling and so the result was more silence and greater suffering.

Episodes in a later chapter reveal both the harm that can result from exposing counter-normative differences that cannot be received and included in the community, and the possibilities for greater coherence that can arise when a community can embrace differences that people bring and include them in the life of the community. She recounts several experiences where she reached out to church pastors for assistance while suffering the post-traumatic effects of rape. Several of her attempts resulted in problematic and unhelpful interactions. One outreach proved to be both positive and healing. While interviewing with a pastor for a ministerial internship required in her seminary curriculum—still experiencing post-traumatic symptoms—she was open about her experience and its effects. Her truth-telling to the pastor was met with acceptance and then included in her ministerial learning process:

17. See chapter 5 for a discussion on masks and covering demands.
18. Coleman, *Bipolar Faith*, 52–53.

"Here's the deal." Talking about rape had become a burden. "Last spring, I was raped. I'm post-traumatic. I don't know until I wake up if it's going to be a good day or a bad day. I don't know how I can contribute to the church. In fact, I really need someone to minister to me. Can you work with that?" My voice contained the weariness and exasperation that I felt. And probably more defensiveness than was appropriate. I was desperate. I had to land somewhere. I also had to be honest about where I was. Nowhere.

"Okay." Reverend Ed didn't move. He didn't lean over to touch and reassure me. He didn't ask me any questions. He didn't suggest a magic formula for getting better. He put the paperwork on his lap, and looked me right in the eyes. "Okay."

"Why don't you just show up when you can? The ministry will find you."

I bit my top lip and blinked my eyes to keep from crying. *Show up when I can. Show up when I can. I can do that. I can do that. I. Can. Do. That.*

I knew then that I would be okay there. This church—or at least this pastor—knew what to do with people who had been victimized: don't ask us for much.

I inhaled and exhaled through my nose. I looked down before I returned his gaze. I smiled. "Okay."[19]

It makes a difference when communities give people—in this instance a community leader in training—the opportunity to include all of who they are and what they bring into the space. It helps to create an opportunity for grace and healing, both for the ones who have been excluded and the ones who now have a richer view of the diversity of human experiences and their connection to the Holy.

In a final example she discovers a renewed faith in God from the experience of accepting and living with her bipolar condition and incorporating it into her faith:

If I can believe—in the midst of my most wordless, painful, razor-shiny moments—that God isn't doing this to me, then that is an act of faith. If I can believe that God hears me, knows me, loves me, and rocks me, then that is a leap of faith. I don't need more than that. I don't need the degrees, the title, the philosophy, the long robes, the approval of my denomination, or special prayers

19. Coleman, *Bipolar Faith*, 183–84.

for sharing the bread and wine. The leap to believe that God does not abandon me is all I need.[20]

This passage at the end of her memoir reveals the movement of her faith experience, born from the disruptive coherence of her truth-telling, and that creates the opportunity for others to find some of their story in her story, thereby, engaging the struggle for justice in the work of acknowledging and embracing the marginalized and disregarded.

Concluding Thoughts

In this chapter I have looked to envision coming out as disruptive coherence as a transformative ethical practice in the struggle for justice. Seeking to make visible, acknowledge, and include the socially excluded others in the midst of our world, I suggested that coming out as disruptive coherence can be a transformative ethical practice of acknowledging and embracing marginalized and disregarded persons, groups and perspectives. Finally, I discussed two possibilities for a concrete praxis of acknowledging and embracing the marginalized and disregarded: (1) create opportunities in communities to profess one's moral conviction of counter-normativity and challenge its exclusion, and (2) create communities that welcome and include multiple identifications of becoming-selfhood-in-relation.

I am left with what feels to me more like an exhortation than a conclusion. Because of the potential of coming out as disruptive coherence—as embodied testimony, as the erotic ethical practice of truth-telling—it ought to be embraced as a transformative practice of justice. In this regard creating opportunities to profess difference and creating communities of inclusion becomes a necessary task of how religious communities live together and open themselves to the many others who they do not yet realize might be in community with them.

As I conclude this book, I reflect on words from Judith Butler about ethical responsibility and truth-telling that have been in the back of my mind over the time that I have worked on this project. Butler crystalizes for me what is at stake in thinking about coming out as a practice of truth-telling: "Perhaps most importantly, we must recognize that ethics requires us to risk ourselves precisely at moments of unknowingness, when what forms us diverges from what lies before us, when our willingness to become

20. Coleman, *Bipolar Faith*, 341–42.

undone in relation to others constitutes our chance of becoming human."[21] With a conviction of religious belief, this willingness to destabilize ourselves and others in order for all to become more fully human is possible because of a confidence in the faithful God who provides the grace needed to courageously embrace disruptive coherence.

21. Butler, *Giving an Account of Oneself*, 136.

Bibliography

Alison, James. *Broken Hearts and New Creations: Intimations of a Great Reversal.* New York: Continuum, 2010.

———. *Faith Beyond Resentment: Fragments Catholic and Gay.* New York: Crossroad, 2001.

Alpert, Rebecca. *Like Bread on the Seder Plate: Jewish Lesbians and the Transformation of Tradition.* New York: Columbia University Press, 1997.

Althaus-Reid, Marcella. *Indecent Theology: Theological Perversions in Sex, Gender and Politics.* New York: Routledge, 2000.

———. "'Let Them Talk . . . !' Doing Liberation Theology from Latin American Closets." In *Liberation Theology and Sexuality,* edited by Marcella Althaus-Reid, 5–17. Burlington, VT: Ashgate, 2006.

———. "Mark." In *The Queer Bible Commentary,* edited by Deryn Guest, et al., 517–25. London: SCM, 2006.

———. *The Queer God.* New York: Routledge, 2003.

Althaus-Reid, Marcella, and Lisa Isherwood, eds. *Trans/Formations.* London: SCM, 2009.

Aponte, Edwin David. *Santo! Varieties of Latino/a Spirituality.* Maryknoll, NY: Orbis, 2012.

Aviv, Caryn S., and David Shneer. *New Jews: The End of the Jewish Diaspora.* New York: New York University Press, 2005.

Ballard, Bruce W. *Understanding MacIntyre.* New York: University Press of America, 2000.

Ballard, Paul. "The Use of Scripture." In *The Wiley-Blackwell Companion to Practical Theology,* edited by Bonnie J. Miller-McLemore, 163–72. Malden, MA: Blackwell, 2012.

Bass, Dorothy C., ed. *Practicing Our Faith: A Way of Life for a Searching People.* San Francisco: Jossey Bass, 2010.

Bass, Dorothy C., and Craig Dykstra, eds. *For Life Abundant: Practical Theology, Theological Education, and Christian Ministry.* Grand Rapids: Eerdmans, 2008.

Bass, Dorothy C., et al. *Christian Practical Wisdom: What It Is, Why It Matters.* Grand Rapids: Eerdmans, 2016.

Battle, Michael. "Liberation." In *The Blackwell Companion to Christian Spirituality,* edited by Arthur Holder, 515–31. Malden, MA: Blackwell, 2005.

Beardsley, Christina, and Michelle O'Brien, eds. *This Is My Body: Hearing the Theology of Transgender Christians.* London: Darton, Longman and Todd, 2016.

Berrú-Davis, Rebecca M. "Theologizing Popular Catholicism." In *The Wiley Blackwell Companion to Latino/a Theology*, edited by Orlando O. Espín, 387–400. New York: Wiley & Sons, 2015.

Bohache, Thomas. "Matthew." In *The Queer Bible Commentary*, edited by Deryn Guest et al., 487–516. London: SCM, 2006.

Boisvert, Donald. "Homosexuality and Spirituality." In *Homosexuality and Religion: An Encyclopedia*, edited by Jeffrey S. Siker, 32–44. Westport, CT: Greenwood, 2007.

Boisvert, Donald L., and Jay Emerson Johnson, eds. *Queer Religion, Volume 1: Homosexuality in Modern Religious History*. Santa Barbara, CA: Praeger, 2012.

———. *Queer Religion, Volume 2: LGBT Movements and Queering Religion*. Santa Barbara, CA: Praeger, 2012.

Bourdieu, Pierre. *Outline of a Theory of Practice*. New York: Cambridge University Press, 1977.

Brock, Rita Nakashima. "Cooking Without Recipes: Interstitial Integrity." In *Off the Menu: Asian and Asian North American Women's Religion & Theology*, edited by Rita Nakashima Brock, et al., 125–44. Louisville, KY: Westminster John Knox, 2007.

———. *Journeys by Heart: A Christology of Erotic Power*. New York: Crossroad, 1988.

Buechel, Andy. *That We Might Become God: The Queerness of Creedal Christianity*. Eugene, OR: Cascade, 2015.

Burrus, Virginia. "Luke-Acts." In *A Postcolonial Commentary on New Testament Writings*, edited by Fernando F. Segovia and R. S. Sujirtharajah, 133–55. London: T. & T. Clark, 2009.

Burrus, Virginia, and Catherine Keller, eds. *Toward a Theology of Eros: Transfiguring Passion at the Limits of Discipline*. New York: Fordham University Press, 2006.

Butler, Judith. *Bodies That Matter*. New York: Routledge, 2011.

———. *Gender Trouble: Feminism and the Subversion of Identity*. New York: Routledge, 1990.

———. *Giving an Account of Oneself*. New York: Fordham University Press, 2005.

———. "Imitation and Gender Insubordination." In *The Lesbian and Gay Studies Reader*, edited by Michele Aina Barale, et al., 307–20. New York: Routledge, 1993.

Cahalan, Kathleen A., and Gordon S. Mikoski, eds. *Opening the Field of Practical Theology: An Introduction*. Lanham, MD: Rowman and Littlefield, 2014.

Cannon, Katie G. "Sexing Black Women: Liberation from the Prisonhouse of Anatomical Authority." In *Loving the Body: Black Religious Studies and the Erotic*, edited by Anthony B. Pinn and Dwight N. Hopkins, 11–30. New York: Palgrave Macmillan, 2004.

Carter, David. *Stonewall: The Riots that Sparked the Gay Revolution*. New York: St. Martin's Griffin, 2010.

Cheng, Patrick S. "Contributions from Queer Theory." In *The Oxford Handbook of Theology, Sexuality, and Gender*, edited by Adrian Thatcher, 153–69. Oxford: Oxford University Press, 2015.

———. *From Sin to Amazing Grace: Discovering the Queer Christ*. New York: Seabury, 2012.

———. *Radical Love: An Introduction to Queer Theology*. New York: Seabury, 2011.

———. *Rainbow Theology: Bridging Race, Sexuality, and Spirit*. New York: Seabury, 2013.

Choi, Jin Young. *Post-Colonial Discipleship of Embodiment: An Asian and Asian American Feminist Reading of the Gospel of Mark*. New York: Palgrave Macmillan, 2015.

Clare, Stephanie D. "'Finally, She's Accepted Herself': Coming Out in Neoliberal Times." *Social Text* 35 (June 2017) 17–38.

Cleaver, Richard. *Know My Name: A Gay Liberation Theology*. Louisville, KY: Westminster John Knox, 1993.

Coleman, Monica A. *Bipolar Faith: A Black Woman's Journey with Depression and Faith*. Minneapolis: Fortress, 2016.

Collins, Patricia Hill. *Black Feminist Thought: Knowledge, Consciousness, and the Politics of Empowerment*. New York: Routledge, 2009.

Collins, Patricia Hill, and Sirma Bilge. *Intersectionality*. Cambridge: Polity, 2016.

Comstock, Gary David. *Gay Theology Without Apology*. Cleveland: Pilgrim, 1993.

Cooper-White, Pamela. "Braided Selves: Theological and Psychological Reflections on 'Core Selves,' Multiplicity, and the Sense of Cohesion." In *Braided Selves: Collected Essays on Multiplicity, God, and Persons*, 195–222. Eugene, OR: Cascade, 2011.

Copeland, M. Shawn. "Body, Representation, and Black Religious Discourse." In *Womanist Theological Ethics: A Reader*, edited by Katie Geneva Cannon, et al., 98–111. Louisville, KY: Westminster John Knox, 2011.

Cornwall, Susannah. *Controversies in Queer Theology*. London: SCM, 2011.

de Certeau, Michel. *The Practice of Everyday Life*. Berkeley: University of California Press, 1984.

De Franza, Megan K. *Sex Difference in Christian Theology: Male, Female, and Intersex in the Image of God*. Grand Rapids: Eerdmans, 2015.

De La Torre, Miguel A. "Confessions of a Latino Macho: From Gay Basher to Gay Ally." In *Out of the Shadows into the Light: Christianity and Homosexuality*, edited by Miguel A. De La Torre, 59–75. St. Louis: Chalice, 2009.

Douglas, Kelly Brown. "Black and Blues: God-Talk/Body Talk for the Black Church." In *Womanist Theological Ethics: A Reader*, edited by Katie Geneva Cannon, et al., 113–31. Louisville, KY: Westminster John Knox, 2011.

———. *Sexuality and the Black Church: A Womanist Perspective*. Maryknoll, NY: Orbis, 1999.

———. *What's Faith Got to Do with It? Black Bodies/Christian Souls*. Maryknoll, NY: Orbis, 2005.

Duberman, Martin. *Stonewall*. New York: Plume, 1994.

Duggan, Lisa. "The New Homonormativity: The Sexual Politics of Neoliberalism." In *Materializing Democracy: Toward a Revised Cultural Politics*, edited by Russ Castronovo and Diane D. Nelson, 175–94. Durham, NC: Duke University Press, 2002.

Dykstra, Craig, and Dorothy C. Bass. "A Theological Understanding of Christian Practices." In *Practicing Theology: Beliefs and Practices in Christian Life*, edited by Miroslav Volf and Dorothy C. Bass, 13–32. Grand Rapids: Eerdmans, 2002.

———. "Times of Yearning, Practices of Faith." In *Practicing Our Faith: A Way of Life for a Searching People*, edited by Dorothy C. Bass, 1–12. San Francisco: Jossey Bass, 2010.

Edman, Elizabeth M. *Queer Virtue: What LGBTQ People Know About Life and Love and How It Can Revitalize Christianity*. Boston: Beacon, 2016.

Eiesland, Nancy L. *The Disabled God: Toward a Liberatory Theology of Disability*. Nashville: Abingdon, 1994.

Ellison, Marvin M. *Erotic Justice: A Liberating Ethic of Sexuality*. Louisville, KY: Westminster John Knox, 1996.

————. *Making Love Just: Sexual Ethics for Perplexing Times*. Minneapolis: Fortress, 2012.

————. "Marriage in a New Key." In *Sexuality and the Sacred: Sources for Theological Reflection*, edited by Marvin M. Ellison and Kelly Brown Douglas, 397–411. Louisville, KY: Westminster John Knox, 2010

————. "Reimagining Good Sex: The Eroticizing of Mutual Respect and Pleasure." In *Sexuality and the Sacred: Sources for Theological Reflection*, edited by Marvin M. Ellison and Kelly Brown Douglas, 245–61. Louisville, KY: Westminster John Knox, 2010.

Farley, Margaret A. *Just Love: A Framework for Christian Sexual Ethics*. New York: Continuum, 2008.

Flunder, Yvette A. *Where the Edge Gathers: Building a Community of Radical Inclusion*. Cleveland: Pilgrim, 2005.

Foucault, Michel. *The Courage of Truth*, edited by Frédéric Gros. New York: Palgrave Macmillan, 2011.

————. *Discipline and Punish: The Birth of the Prison*. New York: Vintage, 1977.

————. *Ethics: Subjectivity and Truth*, edited by Paul Rabinow. New York: New Press, 1997.

————. *The Government of Self and Others*, edited by Frédéric Gros. New York: Palgrave Macmillan, 2010.

————. *The History of Sexuality, Volume I*. New York: Vintage, 1978.

————. *Power/Knowledge: Selected Interviews and Other Writings 1972–1977*, edited by Colin Gordon. New York: Vintage, 1980.

Gerle, Elizabeth. *Passionate Embrace: Luther on Love, Body, and Sensual Presence*. Eugene, OR: Cascade, 2017.

Glaser, Chris. *Coming Out as Sacrament*. Louisville, KY: Westminster John Knox, 1998.

Goldstein, Evan. "The Undoing of Disruption." *The Chronicle of Higher Education*, September 15, 2015. https://www.chronicle.com/article/The-Undoing-of-Disruption /233101.

Goss, Robert. "Gay Erotic Spirituality and the Recovery of Sexual Pleasure." In *Body and Soul: Rethinking Sexuality as Justice-Love*, edited by Marvin M. Ellison and Sylvia Thorson-Smith, 201–16. Cleveland: Pilgrim, 2003.

————. *Jesus Acted Up: A Gay and Lesbian Manifesto*. New York: Harper San Francisco, 1993.

————. "John." In *The Queer Bible Commentary*, edited by Deryn Guest, et al., 548–65. London: SCM, 2006.

————. "Luke." In *The Queer Bible Commentary*, edited by Deryn Guest, et al., 526–47. London: SCM, 2006.

————. *Queering Christ: Beyond Jesus Acted Up*. Cleveland: Pilgrim, 2002.

Goss, Robert E., and Mona West, eds. *Take Back the Word: A Queer Reading of the Bible*. Cleveland: Pilgrim, 2000.

Gramick, Jeannine. "God Shoes." In *Unruly Catholic Nuns: Sisters' Stories*, edited by Jeana del Rosso et al., 14–24. Albany, NY: Excelsior, 2017.

Greenberg, Rabbi Steven. *Wrestling with God and Men: Homosexuality in the Jewish Tradition*. Madison: University of Wisconsin Press, 2004.

Griffin, Horace L. *Their Own Receive Them Not: African American Lesbians and Gays in Black Churches*. Cleveland: Pilgrim, 2006.

Guest, Deryn, et al., eds. *The Queer Bible Commentary*. London: SCM, 2006.

Gula, Richard M. *Moral Discernment*. New York: Paulist, 1997.

Gutiérrez, Gustavo. *We Drink from Our Own Wells: The Spiritual Journey of a People.* Maryknoll, NY: Orbis, 1984.

Halperin, David M. *Saint Foucault: Toward a Gay Hagiography.* New York: Oxford University Press, 1995.

Hames-García, Michael. "What's at Stake in 'Gay Identities'?" In *Identity Politics Reconsidered*, edited by Satya P. Mohany and Paula M. L. Moya, 78–95. New York: Palgrave Macmillan, 2006.

Harker, Richard, et al. *An Introduction to the Work of Pierre Bourdieu: The Practice of Theory.* London: Macmillan, 1990.

Hayes, Diana L. *Forged in the Fiery Furnace: African American Spirituality.* Maryknoll, NY: Orbis, 2012.

———. *No Crystal Stair: Womanist Spirituality.* Maryknoll, NY: Orbis, 2016.

Henderson-Espinoza, Robyn. "Thinking at the Intersections of Theology and the Matrix of Differences: From Intersectionality to Interconnectivity." In *Spotlight on Theological Education Religious Studies News* (April 2015).

Hero, Jakob. "Toward a Queer Theology of Flourishing: Transsexual Embodiment, Subjectivity, and Moral Agency." In *The Bloomsbury Reader in Religion, Sexuality and Gender*, edited by Donald L. Boisvert and Carly Daniel-Hughes, 219–30. New York: Bloomsbury Academic, 2017.

Heyward, Carter. *Touching Our Strength: The Erotic as Power and the Love of God.* San Francisco: Harper and Row, 1989.

Hiddleston, Jane. *Understanding Postcolonialism.* Stocksfield, UK: Acumen, 2009.

Hinze, Bradford E., and Peter C. Phan, eds. *Learning from All the Faithful: A Contemporary Theology of the Sensus Fidei.* Eugene, OR: Pickwick, 2016.

Hopkins, Dwight N. "The Construction of the Black Male Body: Eroticism and Religion." In *Loving the Body: Black Religious Studies and the Erotic*, edited by Anthony B. Pinn and Dwight N. Hopkins, 179–97. New York: Palgrave Macmillan, 2004.

Hoyt, Thomas, Jr. "Testimony." In *Practicing Our Faith: A Way of Life for a Searching People*, edited by Dorothy C. Bass, 89–101. San Francisco: Wiley & Sons, 2010.

Hunt, Mary E. *Fierce Tenderness: A Feminist Theology of Friendship.* Minneapolis: Fortress, 2009.

———. "Sexual Integrity." *Waterwheel: A Quarterly Newsletter of the Women's Alliance for Theology, Ethics and Ritual* 7 (Fall 1994) 1–2.

Isherwood, Lisa. *The Power of Erotic Celibacy: Queering Heteropatriarchy.* New York: T. & T. Clark, 2006.

Isherwood, Lisa, and Elizabeth Stuart. *Introducing Body Theology.* Cleveland: Pilgrim, 1998.

Jakobsen, Janet R., and Ann Pellegrini. *Love the Sin: Sexual Regulation and the Limits of Religious Tolerance.* Boston: Beacon, 2004.

Johnson, Luke Timothy. *The Gospel of Luke.* Collegeville, MN: Liturgical, 1991.

———. *Prophetic Jesus, Prophetic Church.* Grand Rapids: Eerdmans, 2011.

Jordan, Mark D. *Convulsing Bodies: Religion and Resistance in Foucault.* Stanford, CA: Stanford University Press, 2015

———. *The Ethics of Sex.* Malden, MA: Blackwell, 2002.

———. *Teaching Bodies: Moral Formation in the Summa of Thomas Aquinas.* New York: Fordham University Press, 2017.

———. *Telling Truths in Church: Scandal, Flesh, and Christian Speech.* Boston: Beacon, 2003.

Jung, Patricia Beattie, et al., eds. *Good Sex: Feminist Perspectives from the World's Religions.* New Brunswick, NJ: Rutgers University Press, 2001.

Kahl, Brigitte. "Reading Luke Against Luke: Non-Uniformity of Text, Hermeneutics of Conspiracy and 'Scripture Principle' in Luke 1." In *A Feminist Companion to Luke*, edited by Amy-Jill Levine with Marianne Blickenstaff, 70–88. Cleveland: Pilgrim, 2004.

Kamitsuka, Margaret D. "Sexual Pleasure." In *The Oxford Handbook of Theology, Sexuality, and Gender*, edited by Adrian Thatcher, 505–22. Oxford: Oxford University Press, 2015.

Kamitsuka, Margaret D., ed. *The Embrace of Eros: Bodies, Desires, and Sexuality in Christianity.* Minneapolis: Fortress, 2010.

King, Martin Luther, Jr. *Stride Toward Freedom: The Montgomery Story* [1958]. Boston: Beacon, 2010.

Kotz, Liz. "The Body You Want: Liz Kotz Interviews Judith Butler." *Artforum* (November 1992) 82–89.

Knight, Kelvin, ed. *The MacIntyre Reader.* Cambridge: Polity, 1988.

Kugle, Scott Siraj al-Haqq. *Homosexuality in Islam: Critical Reflection on Gay, Lesbian, and Transgender Muslims.* London: Oneworld, 2010.

———. *Living Out Islam: Voices of Gay, Lesbian, and Transgender Muslims.* New York: New York University Press, 2014.

Kundtz, David J., and Bernard S. Schlager. *Ministry Among God's Queer Folk: LGBT Pastoral Care.* Cleveland: Pilgrim, 2007.

Kwok, Pui-lan. "Asian and Asian American Churches." In *Homosexuality and Religion: An Encyclopedia*, edited by Jeffrey S. Siker, 59–62. Westport, CT: Greenwood, 2007.

———. "Body and Pleasure in Postcoloniality." In *Dancing Theology in Fetish Boots: Essays in Honor of Marcella Althaus-Reid*, edited by Lisa Isherwood and Mark D. Jordan, 31–43. London: SCM, 2010.

Ladin, Joy. *Through the Door of Life: A Jewish Journey Between Genders.* Madison: University of Wisconsin Press, 2012.

Lepore, Jill. "The Disruption Machine: What the Gospel of Innovation Gets Wrong." *The New Yorker*, June 23, 2014.

Levine, Amy-Jill. "Introduction." In *A Feminist Companion to Luke*, edited by Amy-Jill Levine with Marianne Blickenstaff, 1–22. Cleveland: Pilgrim, 2004.

Lightsey, Pamela R. *Our Lives Matter: A Womanist Queer Theology.* Eugene, OR: Pickwick, 2015.

Long, Ronald E. "One Gay Man's Trinitarian Faith." In *Queer Religion: Homosexuality in Modern Religious History, Volume 1*, edited by Donald L. Boisvert and Jay Emerson Johnson, 215–30. Santa Barbara, CA: Praeger, 2012.

Long, Thomas G. *Testimony: Talking Ourselves into Being Christian.* San Francisco: Jossey Bass, 2004.

Lorde, Audre. *Sister Outsider.* Trumansburg, NY: Crossing, 1984.

Loughlin, Gerard. "Introduction: The End of Sex." In *Queer Theology: Rethinking the Western Body*, edited by Gerard Loughlin, 1–34. Malden: Blackwell, 2007.

Loughlin, Gerard, ed. *Queer Theology: Rethinking the Western Body.* Malden: Blackwell, 2007.

Lutz, Christopher Stephen. *Reading Alasdair MacIntyre's 'After Virtue'.* New York: Continuum International, 2012.

Lynch, Richard A. "Discourse." In *The Cambridge Foucault Lexicon*, edited by Leonard Lawlor and John Nale, 120–25. New York: Cambridge University Press, 2014.

MacIntyre, Alasdair. *After Virtue: A Study in Moral Theory*. Notre Dame: University of Notre Dame Press, 1984.

Massingale, Brian N. "Beyond 'Who Am I to Judge?': The *Sensus Fidelium*, LGBT Experience, and Truth-Telling in the Church." In *Learning from All the Faithful: A Contemporary Theology of the* Sensus Fidei, edited by Bradford E. Hinze and Peter C. Phan, 170–83. Eugene, OR: Pickwick, 2016.

McCall, Corey. "Parresia." In *The Cambridge Foucault Lexicon*, edited by Leonard Lawlor and John Nale, 334–36. New York: Cambridge University Press, 2014.

McCarty, Richard W. *Sexual Virtue: An Approach to Contemporary Christian Ethics*. Albany, NY: SUNY, 2015.

McHoul, Alec, and Wendy Grace. *A Foucault Primer: Discourse, Power and the Subject*. Melbourne, Australia: Melbourne University Press, 1993.

McIntosh, Mark A. *Discernment and Truth: The Spirituality and Theology of Knowledge*. New York: Crossroad, 2004.

McLaren, Margaret A. "Desire." In *The Cambridge Foucault Lexicon*, edited by Leonard Lawlor and John Nale, 99–101. New York: Cambridge University Press, 2014.

McNeill, John J. *Both Feet Firmly Planted in Midair: My Spiritual Journey*. Louisville, KY: Westminster John Knox, 1998.

———. *The Church and the Homosexual, Third Edition*. Boston: Beacon, 1988.

———. *Freedom, Glorious Freedom: The Spiritual Journey to the Fullness of Life for Gays, Lesbians, and Everybody Else*. Boston: Beacon, 1995.

———. *Sex As God Intended*. Maple Shade, NJ: Lethe, 2008.

———. *Taking a Chance on God: Liberating Theology for Gays, Lesbians, and their Lovers, Families, and Friends*. Boston: Beacon, 1988.

Michaelson, Jay. *God vs. Gay? The Religious Case for Equality*. Boston: Beacon, 2011.

Miller-McLemore, Bonnie J. *Christian Theology in Practice: Discovering a Discipline*. Grand Rapids: Eerdmans, 2012.

Miller-McLemore, Bonnie J., ed. *The Wiley-Blackwell Companion to Practical Theology*. Malden, MA: Blackwell, 2012.

Mollenkott, Virginia Ramey. *Omnigender: a Trans-religious Approach*. Cleveland: Pilgrim, 2007.

Mollenkott, Virginia Ramey, and Vanessa Sheridan. *Transgender Journeys*. Cleveland: Pilgrim, 2003.

Monroe, Irene. "Between a Rock and a Hard Place: Struggling with the Black Church's Heterosexism and the White Queer Community's Racism." In *Out of the Shadows into the Light: Christianity and Homosexuality*, edited by Miguel A. De La Torre, 39–58. St. Louis: Chalice, 2009.

———. "When and Where I Enter, Then the Whole Race Enters with Me: Que(e)rying Exodus." In *Take Back the Word: A Queer Reading of the Bible*, edited by Robert E. Goss and Mona West, 82–91. Cleveland: Pilgrim, 2000.

Morris, Stephen. *"When Brothers Dwell in Unity": Byzantine Christianity and Homosexuality*. Jefferson: McFarland, 2016.

Muers, Rachel. "The Ethics of Stats: Some Contemporary Questions About Telling the Truth." *Journal of Religious Ethics* 42 (March 2014) 1–21.

———. *Testimony: Quakerism and Theological Ethics*. London: SCM, 2015.

Mullins, Michael. *The Gospel of Luke: a Commentary*. Dublin: Columba, 2010.

Nouwen, Henri J. M., with Michael J. Christensen and Rebecca J. Laird. *Discernment: Reading the Signs of Daily Life.* New York: HarperOne, 2013.

O'Neill, Craig, and Kathleen Ritter. *Coming Out Within: Stages of Spiritual Awakening for Lesbians and Gay Men.* San Francisco: Harper San Francisco, 1992.

Pak, Su Yon. "Coming Home/Coming Out: Reflections of a Queer Family and the Challenge of Eldercare in the Korean Diaspora." *Theology and Sexuality* 17 (2011) 337–52.

———. "I's Wide Shut: Eyelid Surgery as a Window into the Spirituality of Korean American Adolescent Girls." In *The Sacred Selves of Adolescent Girls: Hard Stories of Race, Class, and Gender,* edited by Evelyn L. Parker, 15–42. Cleveland: Pilgrim, 2006.

Pak, Su Yon, et al. *Singing the Lord's Song in a New Land: Korean American Practices of Faith.* Louisville, KY: Westminster John Knox, 2005.

Paulsell, Stephanie. "Honoring the Body." In *Practicing Our Faith: A Way of Life for a Searching People,* edited by Dorothy C. Bass, 13–28. San Francisco: Jossey Bass, 2010.

———. *Honoring the Body: Meditations on a Christian Practice.* San Francisco: Jossey Bass, 2002.

Peckruhn, Heike. *Meaning in Our Bodies: Sensory Experience as Constructive Theological Imagination.* Oxford: Oxford University Press, 2017.

Pinn, Antony B., and Dwight N. Hopkins, eds. *Loving the Body: Black Religious Studies and the Erotic.* New York: Palgrave Macmillan, 2004.

Puar, Jasbir K. *Terrorist Assemblages: Homonationalism in Queer Times.* Durham, NC: Duke University Press, 2007.

Ramsay, Nancy. "Intersectionality and Theological Education." In *Spotlight on Theological Education Religious Studies News* (April 2015). http://rsn.aarweb.org/spotlight-on/ theo-ed/intersectionality/intersectionality-and-theological-education.

Rasmussen, Larry. "Shaping Communities." In *Practicing Our Faith: A Way of Life for a Searching People,* edited by Dorothy C. Bass, 117–30. San Francisco: Jossey Bass, 2010.

Rogers, Eugene F., Jr. "Bodies Demand Language: Thomas Aquinas." In *Queer Theology: Rethinking the Western Body,* edited by Gerard Loughlin, 176–87. Malden, MA: Blackwell, 2007.

———. *Sexuality and the Christian Body: Their Way into the Triune God.* Oxford: Blackwell, 1999.

Rogers, Frank, Jr. "Discernment." In *Practicing Our Faith: A Way of Life for a Searching People,* edited by Dorothy C. Bass, 103–116. San Francisco: Jossey Bass, 2010.

Rudy, Kathy. *Sex and the Church: Gender, Homosexuality, and the Transformation of Christian Ethics.* Boston: Beacon, 1997.

Sanders, Cody J., and Angela Yarber. *Microaggressions in Ministry: Confronting the Hidden Violence of Everyday Church.* Louisville, KY: Westminster John Knox, 2015.

Sedgwick, Eve Kosofsky. *Epistemology of the Closet.* Berkeley: University of California Press, 1990.

Sheppard, Phillis Isabella. *Self, Culture, and Others in Womanist Practical Theology.* New York: Palgrave Macmillan, 2011.

Shneer, David, and Caryn Aviv, eds. *Queer Jews.* New York: Routledge, 2002.

Shore-Goss, Robert E. "The Holy Spirit as Mischief-Maker." In *Queering Christianity: Finding a Place at the Table for LGBTQI Christians,* edited by Robert E. Shore-Goss, et al., 97–119. Santa Barbara, CA: Praeger, 2013.

Shore-Goss, Robert E., et al., eds. *Queering Christianity: Finding a Place at the Table for LGBTQI Christians*. Santa Barbara, CA: Praeger, 2013.

Shults, F. Le Ron, and Jan-Olav Henriksen, eds. *Saving Desire: The Seduction of Christian Theology*. Grand Rapids: Eerdmans, 2011.

Snider, Phil, ed. *Justice Calls: Sermons of Welcome and Affirmation*. Eugene, OR: Cascade, 2016.

Stone, Brad. "Practice." In *The Cambridge Foucault Lexicon*, edited by Leonard Lawlor and John Nale, 386–91. New York: Cambridge University Press, 2014.

Stuart, Elizabeth. *Gay and Lesbian Theologies: Repetitions with Critical Difference*. Burlington: Ashgate, 2003.

Sullivan, Nikki. *A Critical Introduction to Queer Theory*. New York: New York University Press, 2003.

Talvacchia, Kathleen T. *Critical Minds and Discerning Hearts: A Spirituality of Multicultural Teaching*. St. Louis: Chalice, 2003.

———. "Disrupting the Theory-Practice Binary." In *Queer Christianities: Lived Religion in Transgressive Forms*, edited by Kathleen T. Talvacchia, et al., 184–94. New York: New York University Press, 2015.

Talvacchia, Kathleen T., et al., eds. *Queer Christianities: Lived Religion in Transgressive Forms*. New York: New York University Press, 2015.

Tanis, Justin. *Trans-Gendered: Theology, Ministry and Communities of Faith*. Cleveland: Pilgrim, 2003.

Tanner, Kathryn. "Theological Reflection and Christian Practices." In *Practicing Theology: Beliefs and Practices in Christian Life*, edited by Miroslav Volf and Dorothy C. Bass, 228–42. Grand Rapids: Eerdmans, 2002.

Taylor, Chloë. *The Routledge Guidebook to Foucault's The History of Sexuality*. New York: Routledge, 2017.

Thatcher, Adrian, ed. *The Oxford Handbook of Theology, Sexuality, and Gender*. Oxford: Oxford University Press, 2015.

Thurman, Howard. *Jesus and the Disinherited*. Boston: Beacon, 1996.

Townes, Emile M. "Ethics as an Art of Doing the Work Our Souls Must Have." In *Womanist Theological Ethics: A Reader*, edited by Katie Geneva Cannon et al., 35–50. Louisville, KY: Westminster John Knox, 2011.

———. *In a Blaze of Glory: Womanist Spirituality as Social Witness*. Nashville: Abingdon, 1995.

Usog, Carmelita. "Women's Spirituality for Justice." In *Hope Abundant: Third World and Indigenous Women's Theology*, edited by Kwok Pui-lan, 255–66. Maryknoll, NY: Orbis, 2010.

Volf, Miroslav, and Dorothy C. Bass, eds. *Practicing Theology: Beliefs and Practices in Christian Life*. Grand Rapids: Eerdmans, 2001.

Webb, Jenn, et al., eds. *Understanding Bourdieu*. Thousand Oaks, CA: Sage, 2002.

Wilchins, Riki Anne. "What Does It Cost to Tell the Truth?" In *The Transgender Studies Reader*, Volume 1, edited by Susan Stryker and Stephen Whittle, 547–51. New York: Taylor and Francis, 2006.

Wilcox, Melissa M. *Coming Out in Christianity: Religion, Identity and Community*. Bloomington: Indiana University Press, 2003.

Wilkerson, William S. "Is There Something You Need to Tell Me? Coming Out and the Ambiguity of Experience." In *Reclaiming Identity: Realist Theory and the Predicament of Post-Modernism*, edited by Paula M.L Moya and Michael R. Hames-García, 251–78. Berkeley, CA: University of California Press, 2000.

Wolfteich, Claire E., ed. *Invitation to Practical Theology: Catholic Voices and Visions*. New York: Paulist, 2014.

Yoshino, Kenji. *Covering: The Hidden Assault on Our Civil Rights*. New York: Random House, 2006.

Young, Thelathia Nikki. *Black Queer Ethics, Family, and Philosophical Imagination*. New York: Palgrave Macmillan, 2016.

Zimman, Lal. "The Other Kind of Coming Out: Transgender People and the Coming Out Narrative Genre." *Gender and Language* 3 (2009) 53–80.